SPACEIMAGES

THESE IMAGES, FROM JPL/NASA WERE FIRST
PRESENTED AT AN EXHIBITION AT THE GREY ART
GALLERY AND STUDY CENTER, NEW YORK UNIVERSITY:
THE PHOTOGRAPHY OF SPACE EXPLORATION,
SUMMER 1981. THE EXPOSITION WAS ORGANIZED BY
ROBERT R. LITTMAN, DIRECTOR AND RICHARD
MAURER, GUEST CURATOR.

PUBLISHED IN THE UNITED STATES OF AMERICA BY
LUSTRUM PRESS, INC., BOX 450, CANAL STREET
STATION, NEW YORK CITY, 10013.

JOHN FLATTAU, RALPH GIBSON AND ARNE LEWIS
DESIGNED BY ARNE LEWIS
TYPOGRAPHY BY MKP, INC.
PRINTED BY RAPOPORT PRINTING CORPORATION, N.Y.
BOUND BY SENDOR BINDERY, INC., N.Y.
MANUFACTURED IN THE UNITED STATES OF AMERICA
LIBRARY OF CONGRESS CATALOG CARD NUMBER: 81-84668
ISBN: 0-912810-36-X (PAPER) 0-912810-37-8 (HARDCOVER)

VACUUM

LUSTRUM PRESS

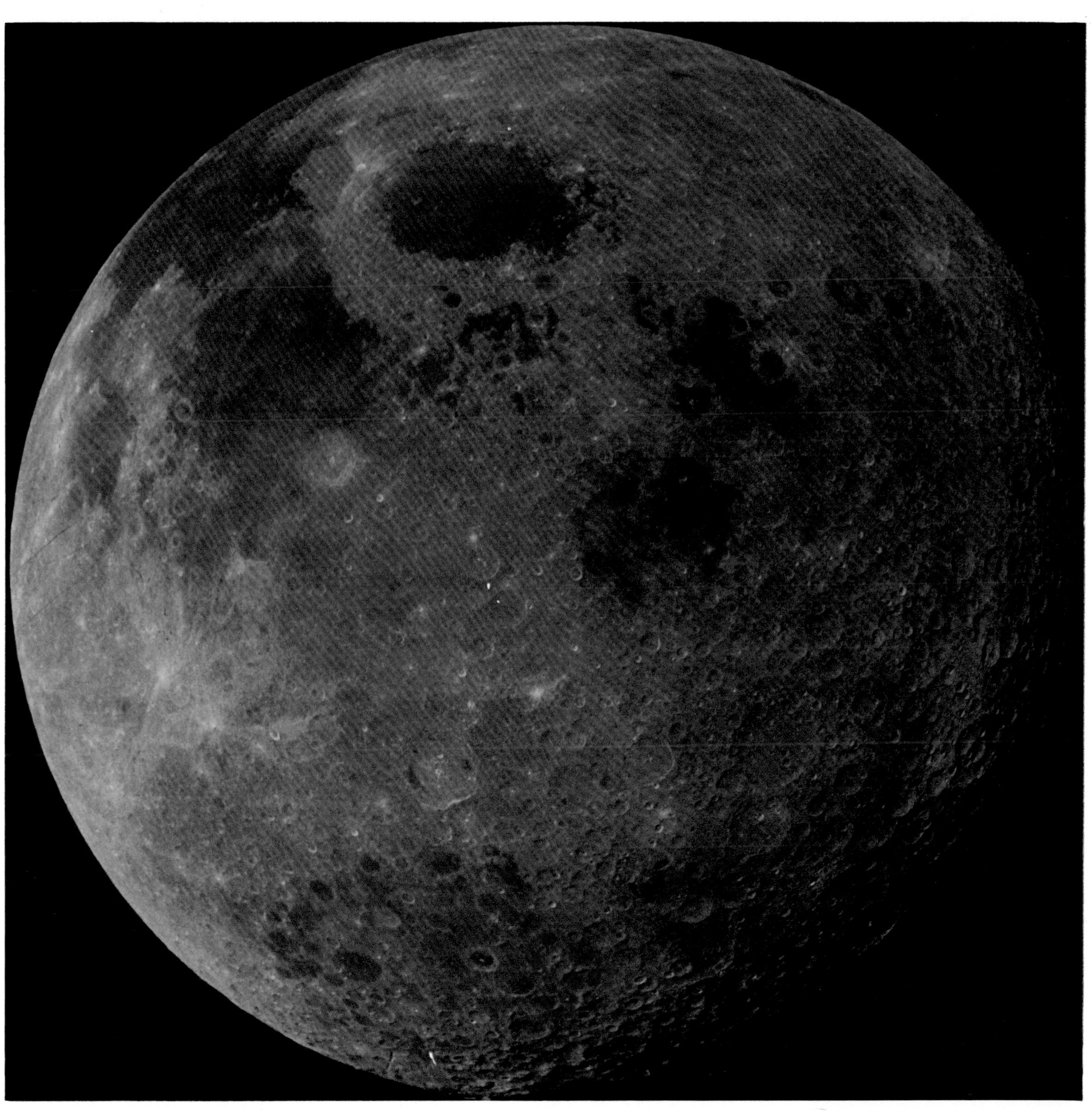

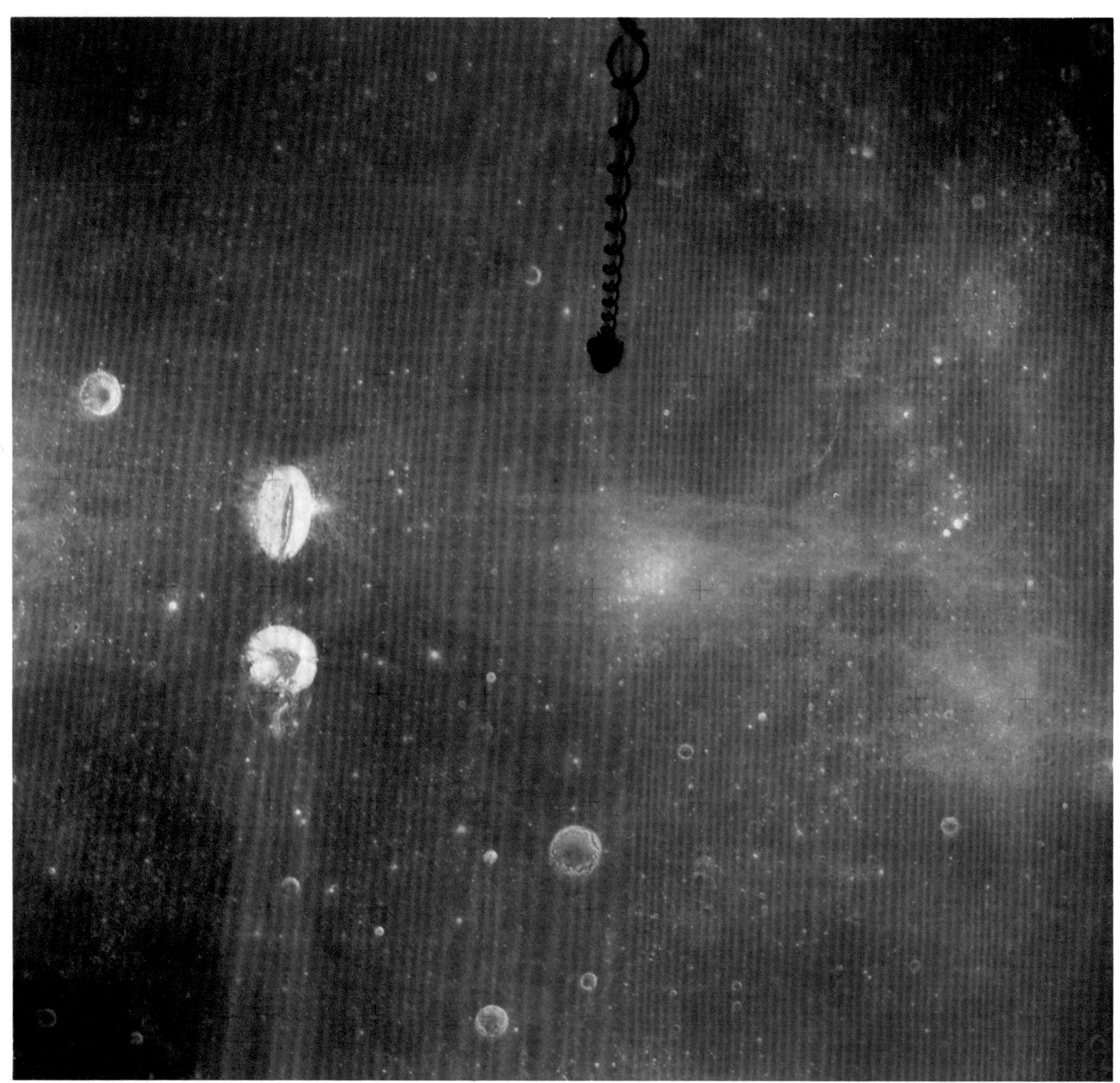

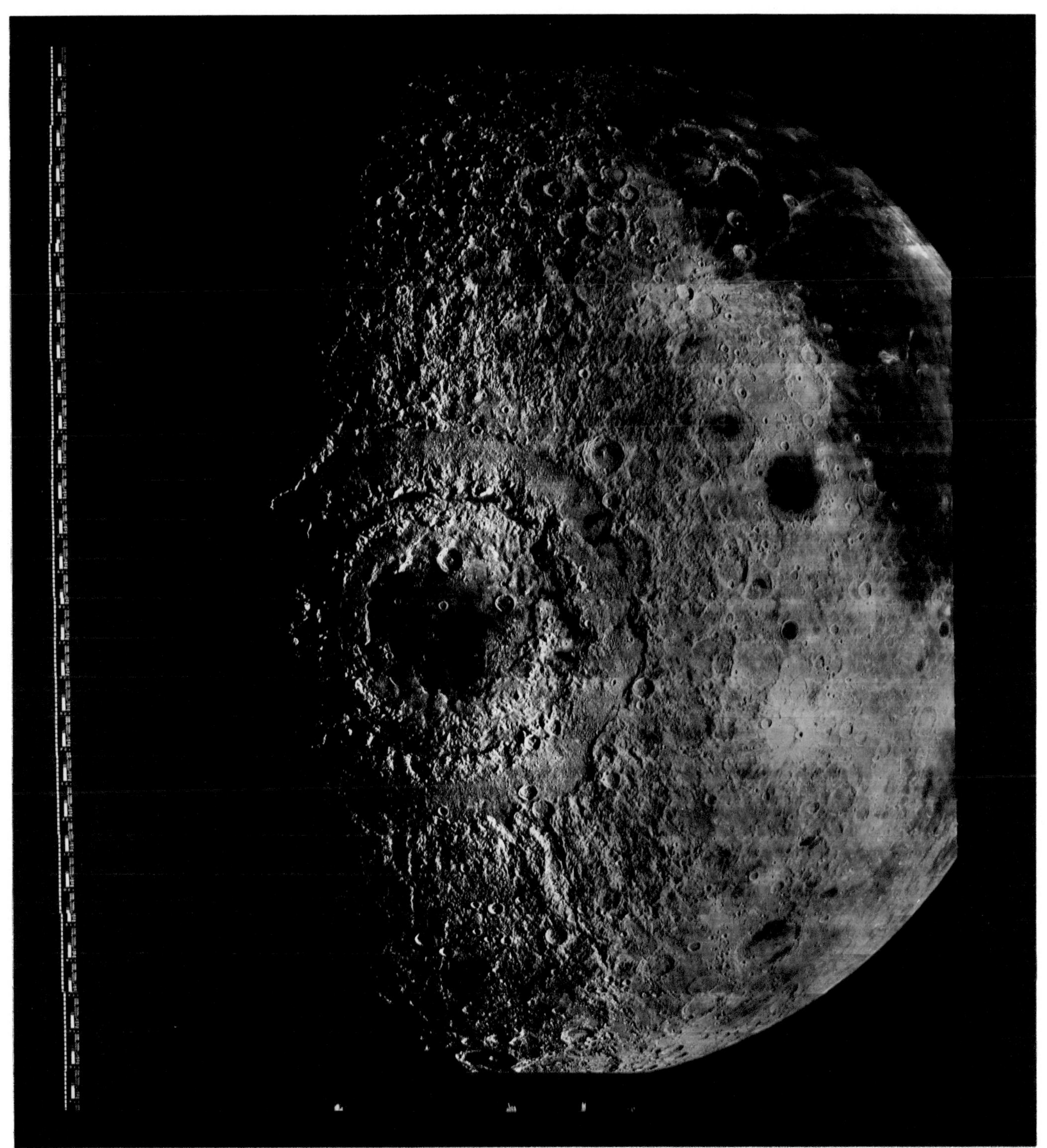

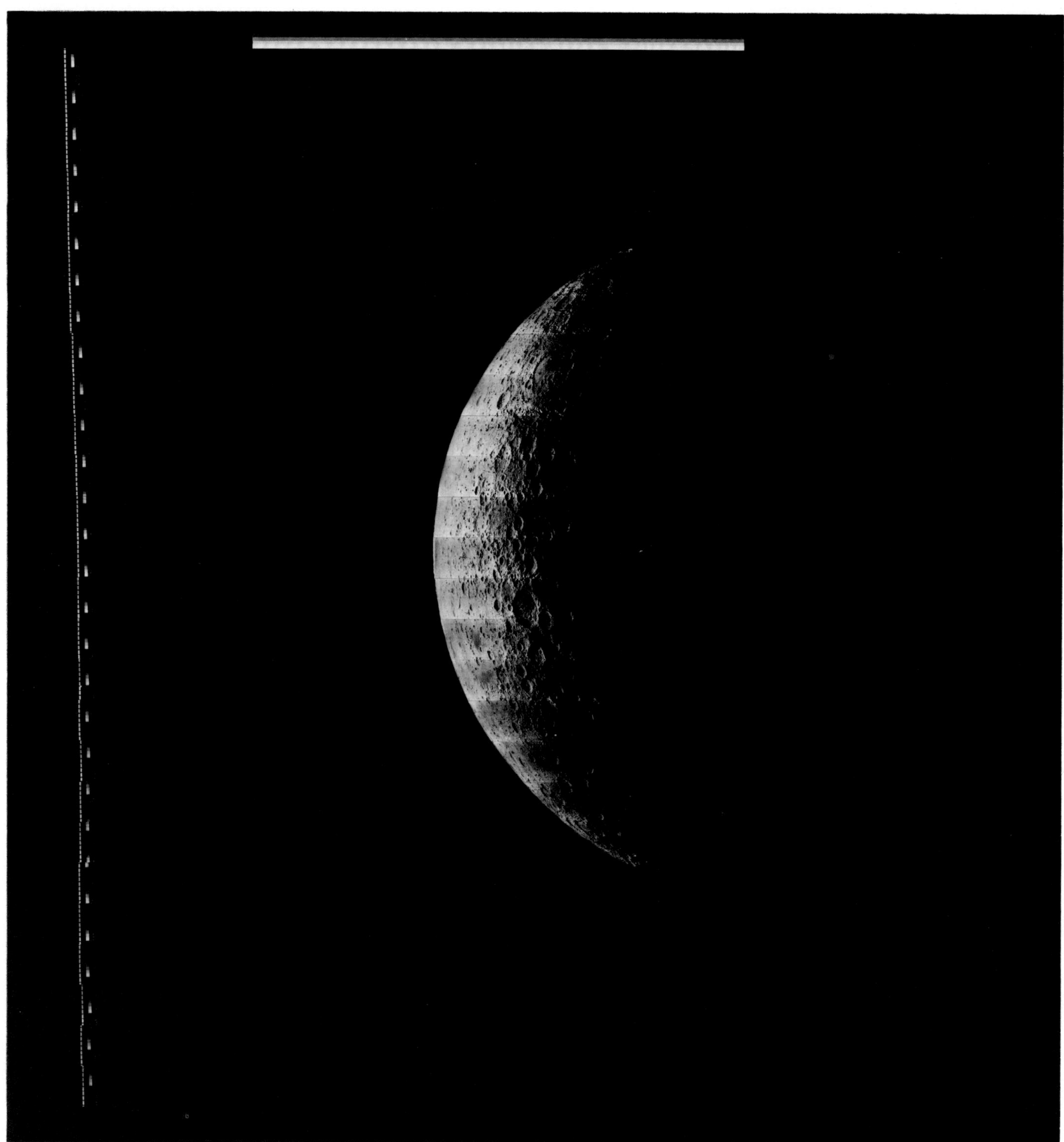

 MOON FROM 3000 MILES

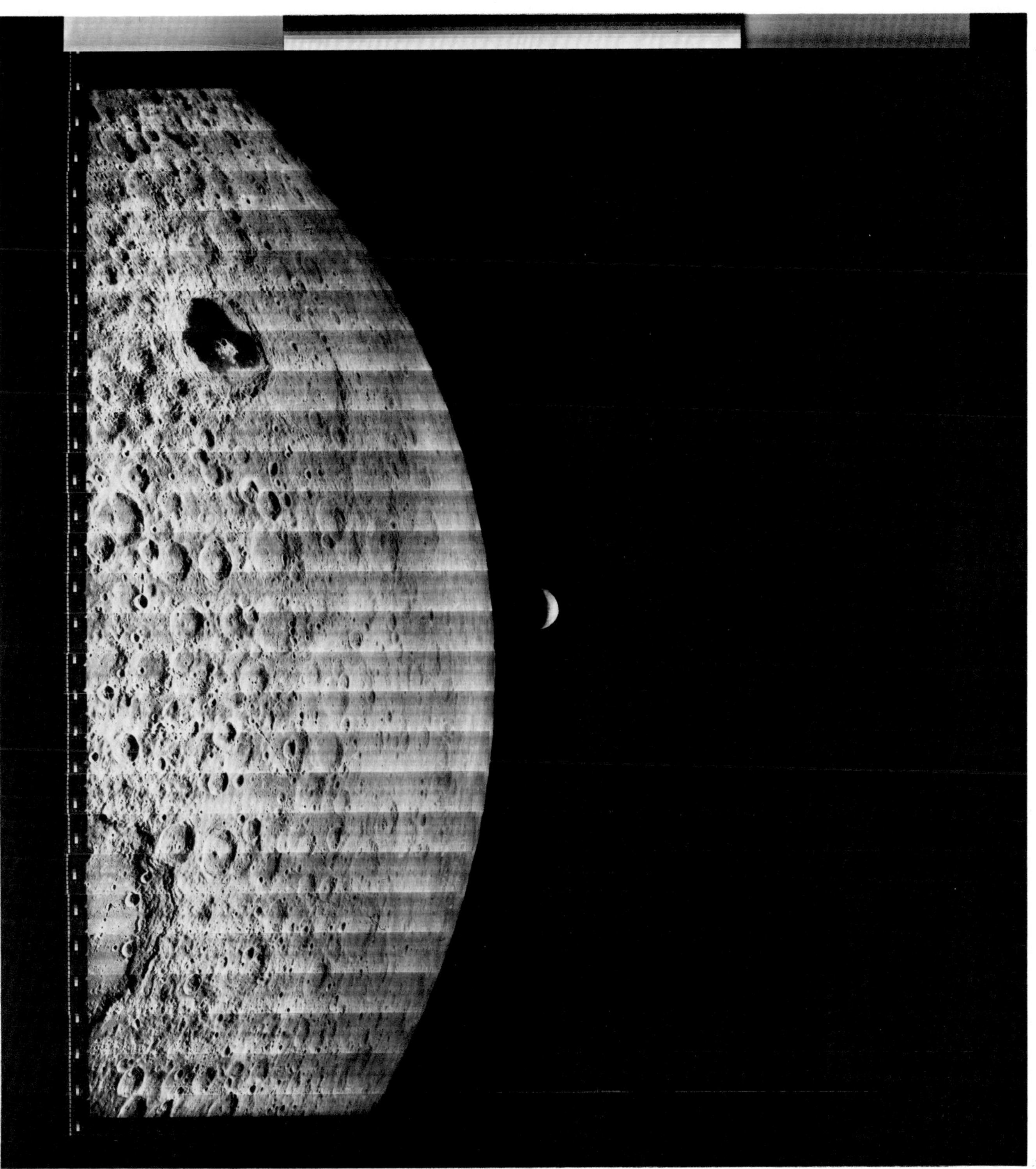

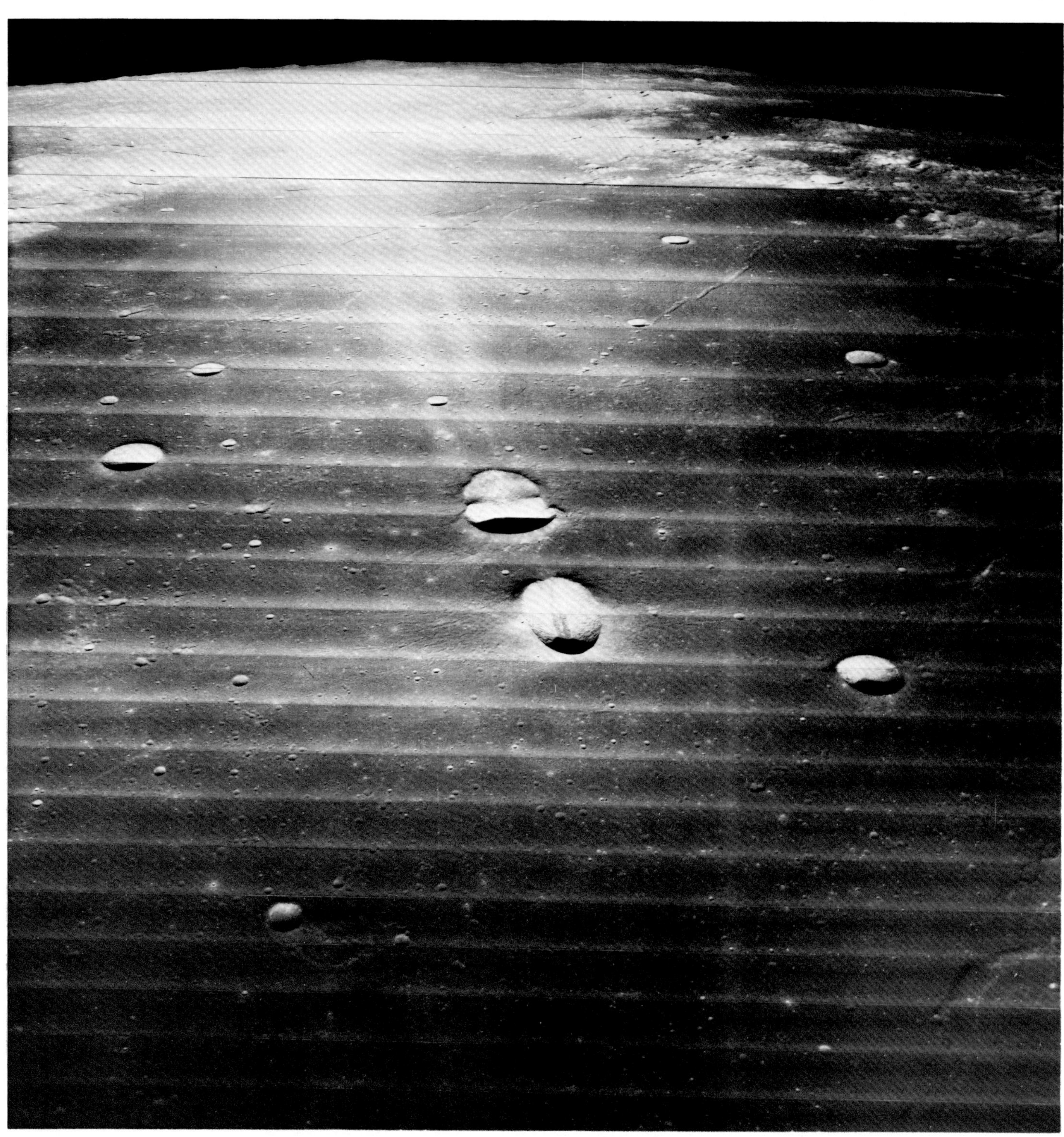

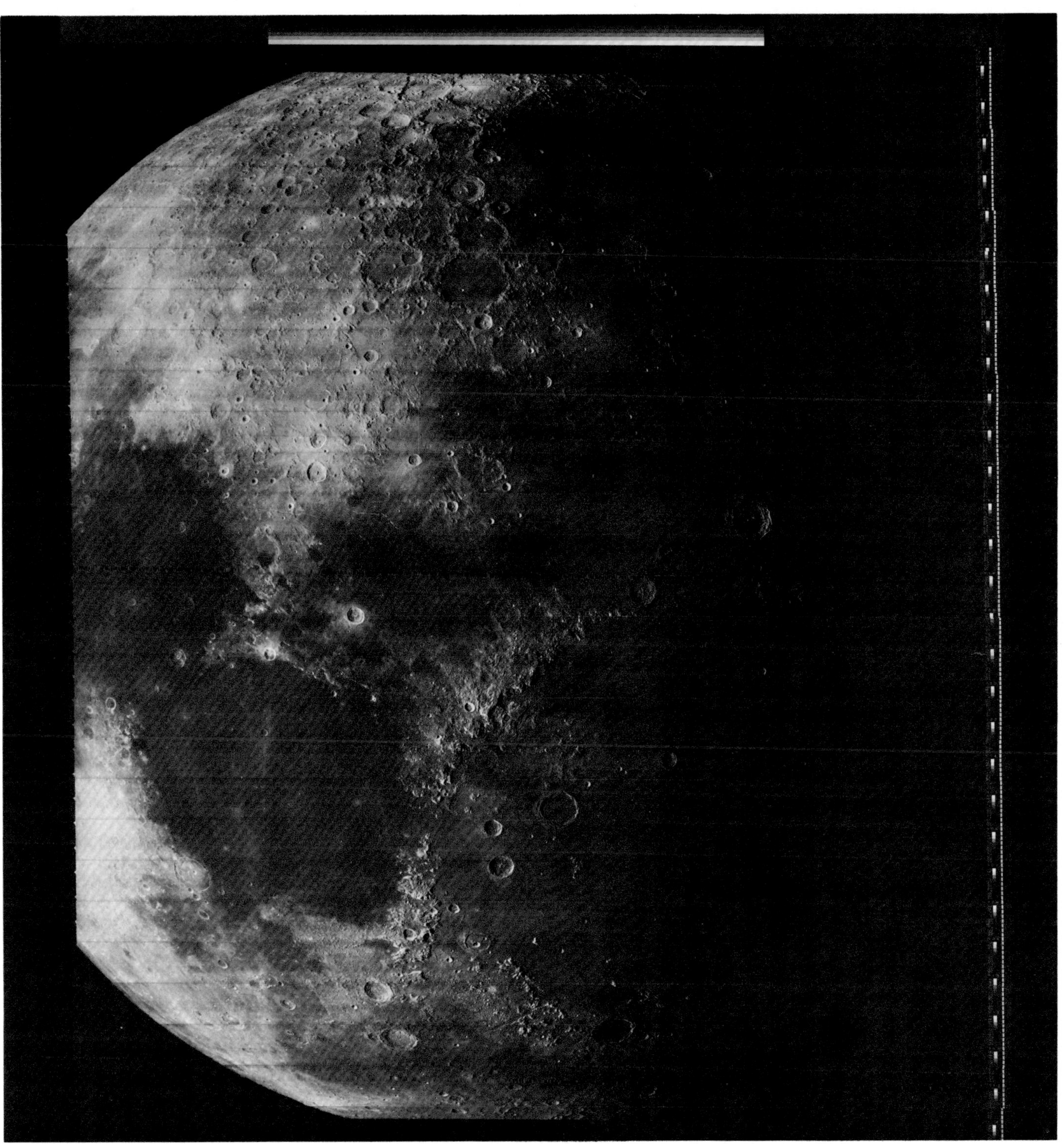

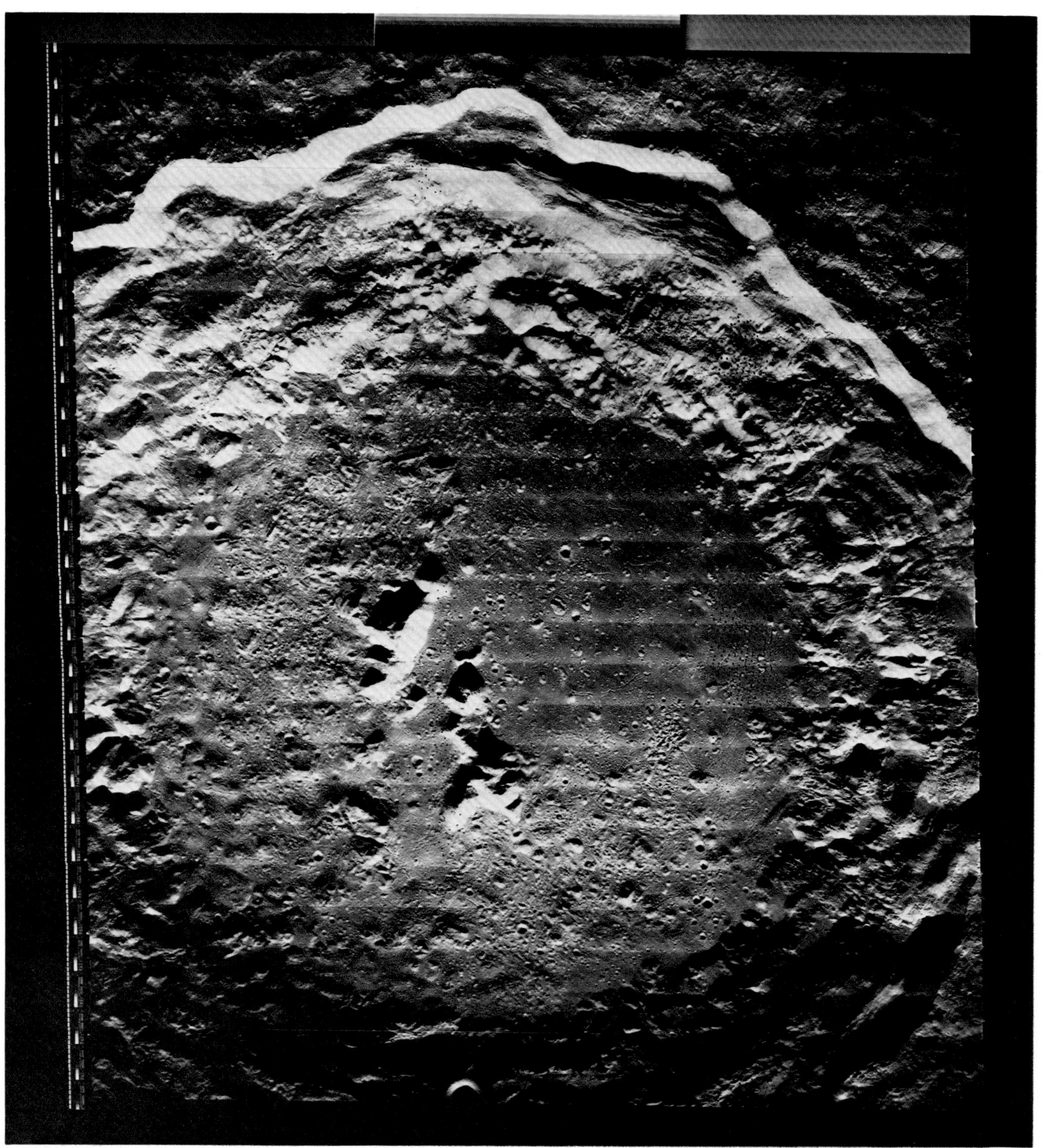

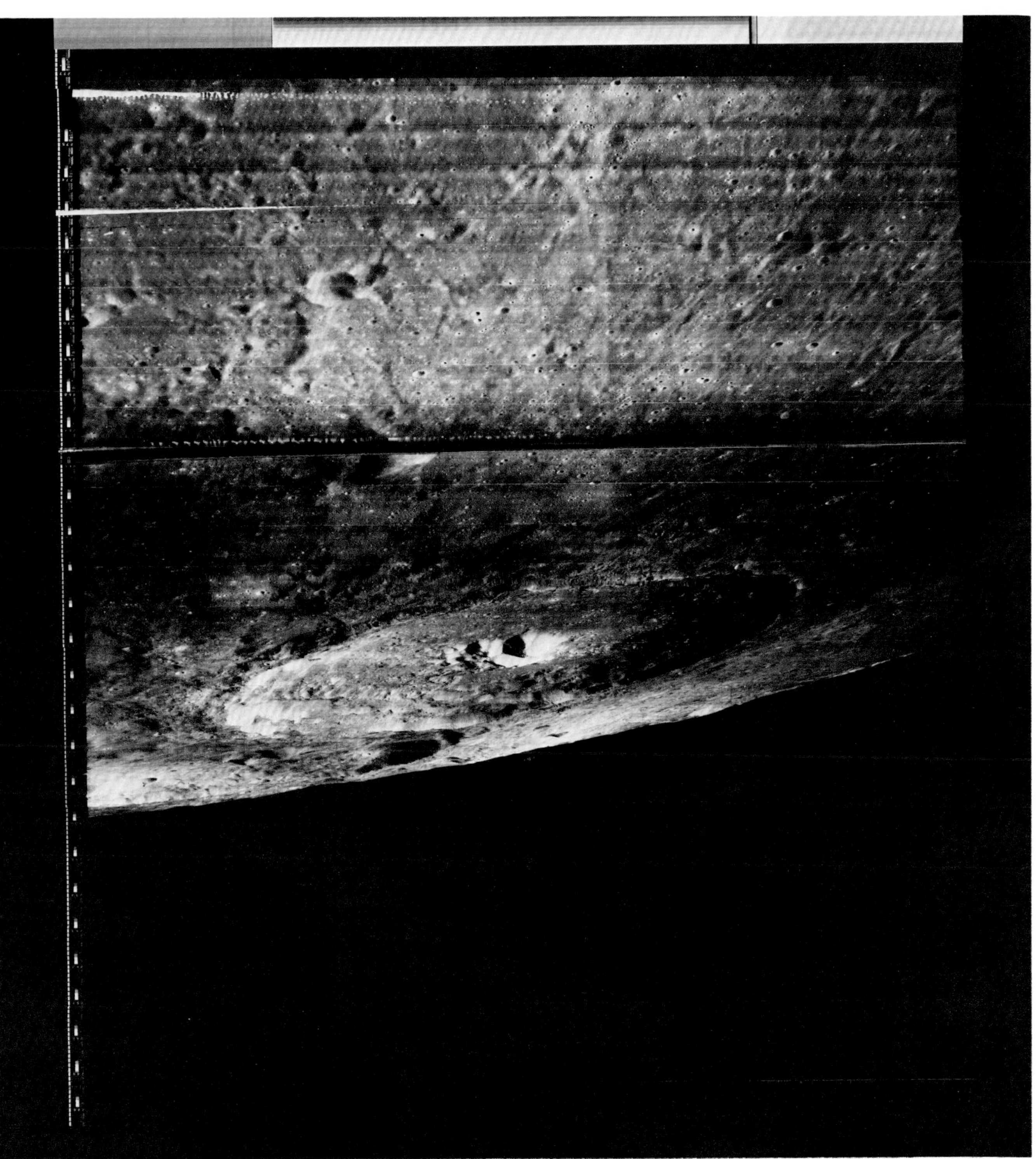

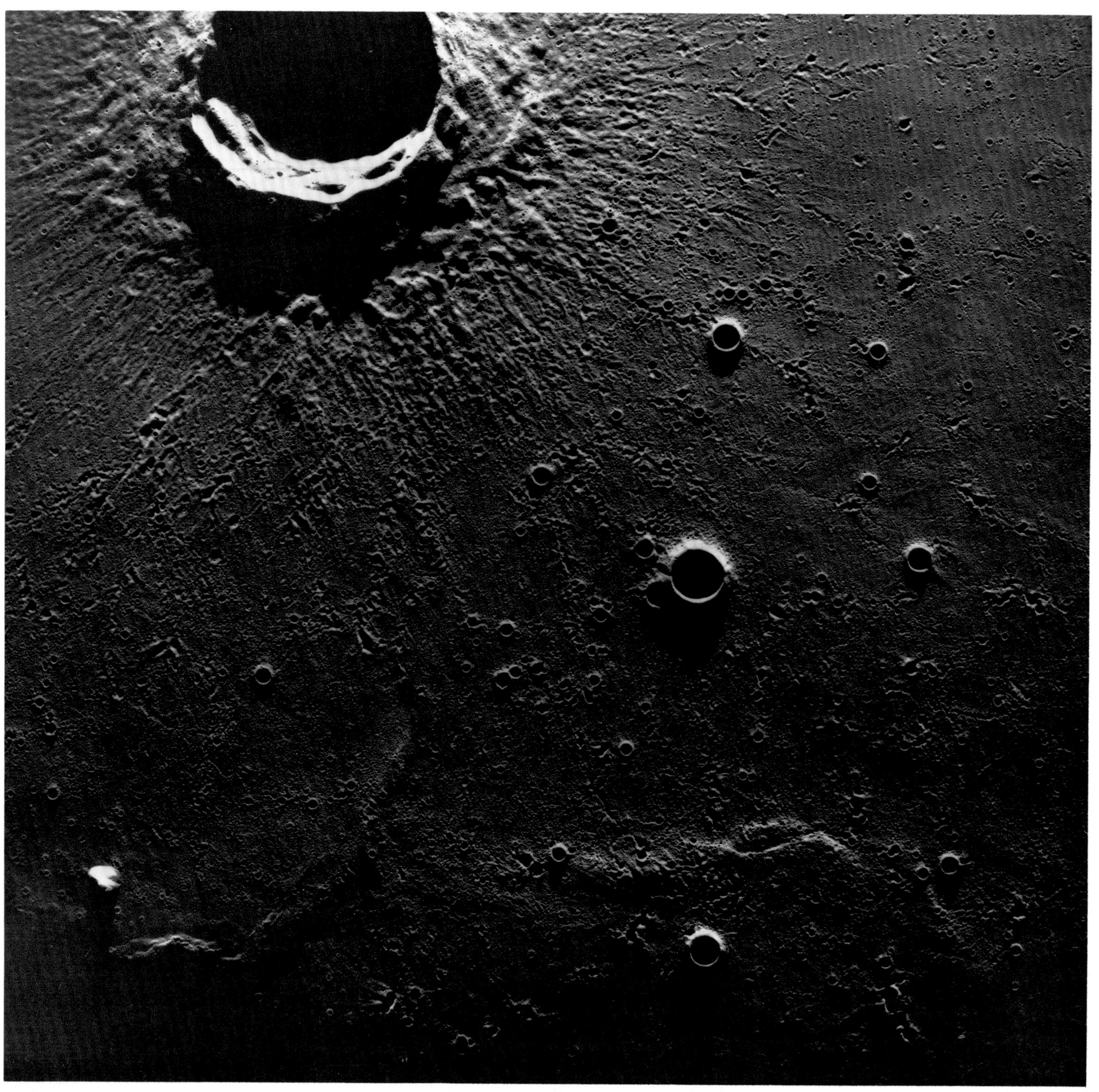

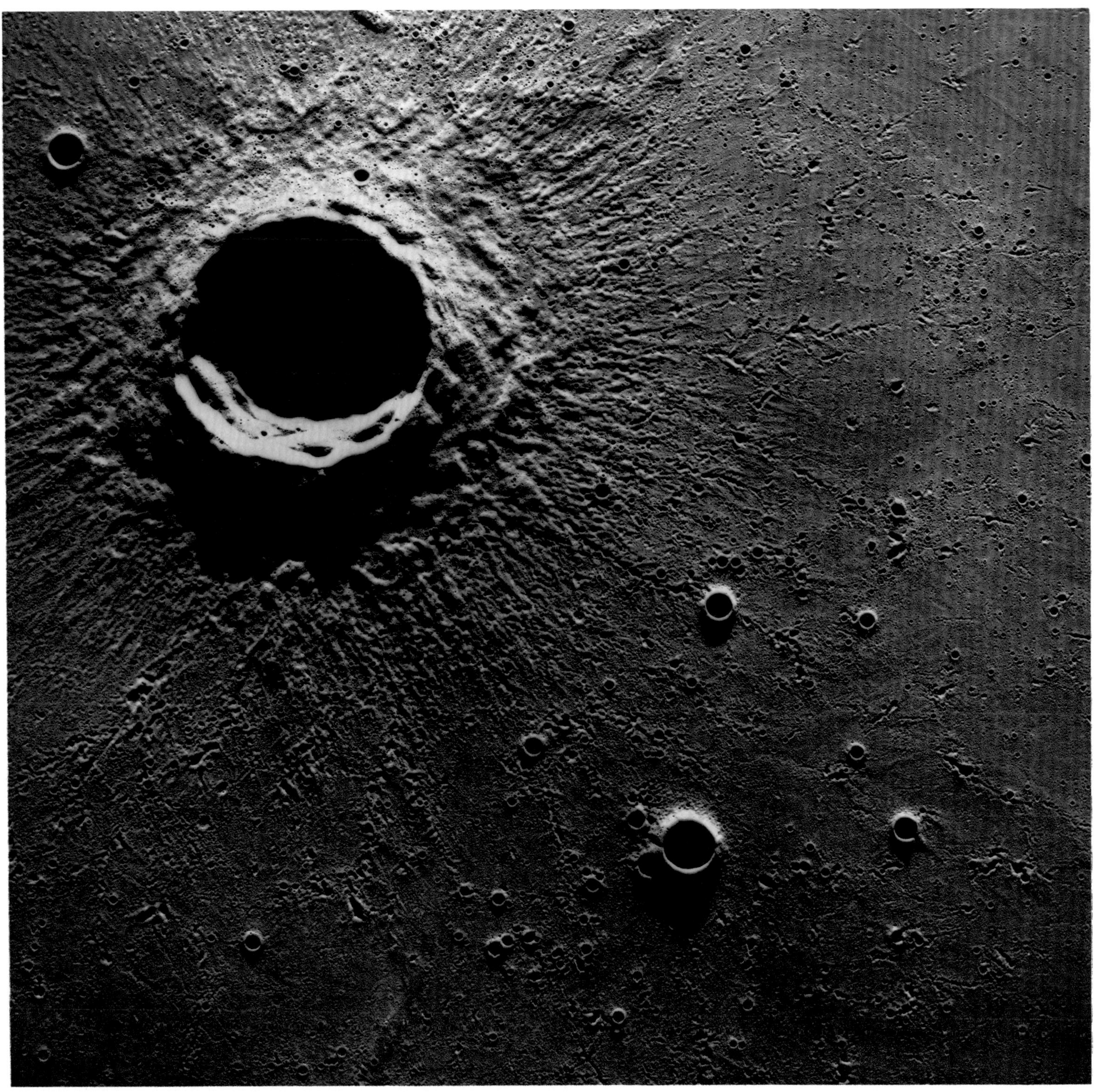

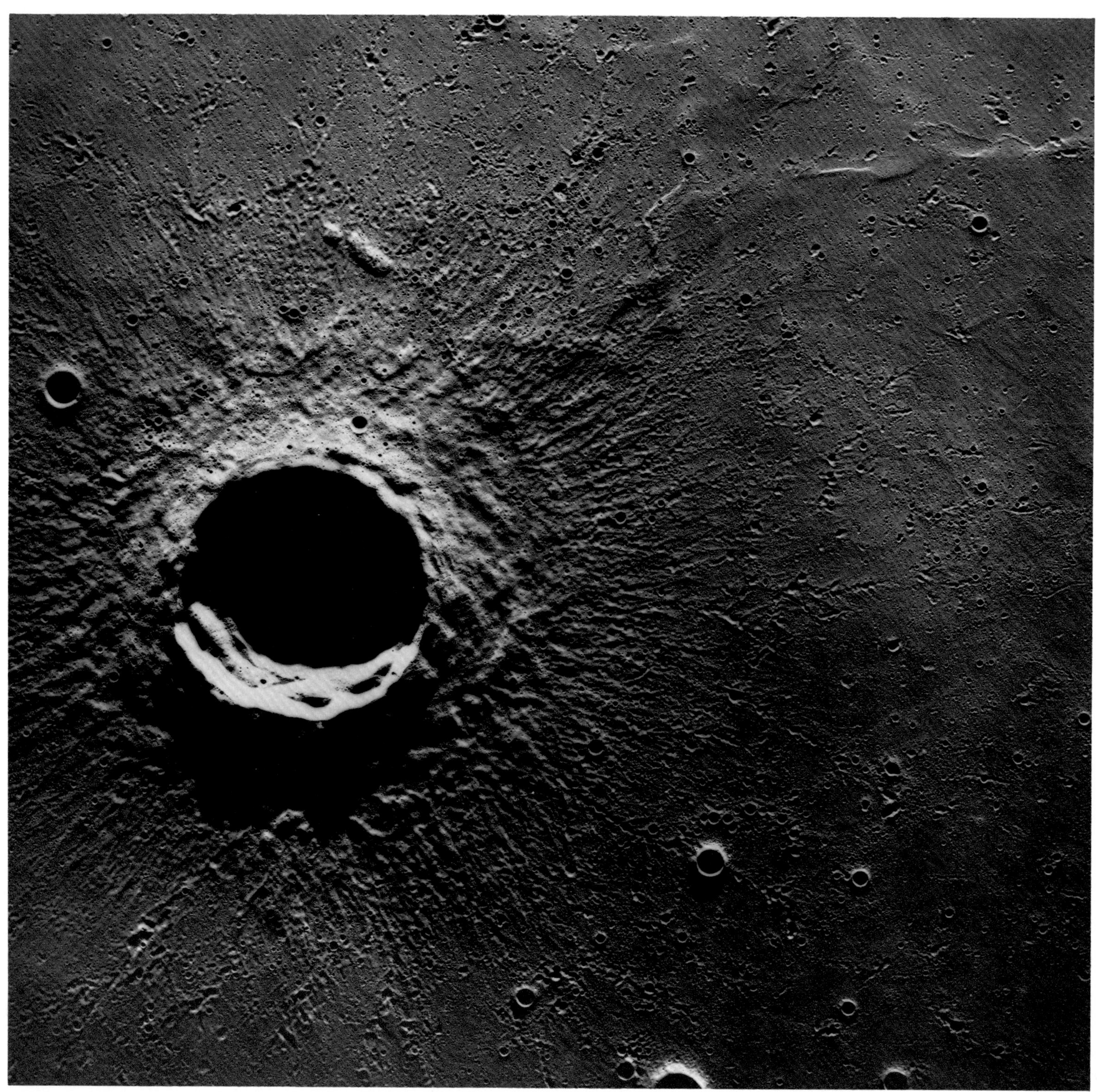

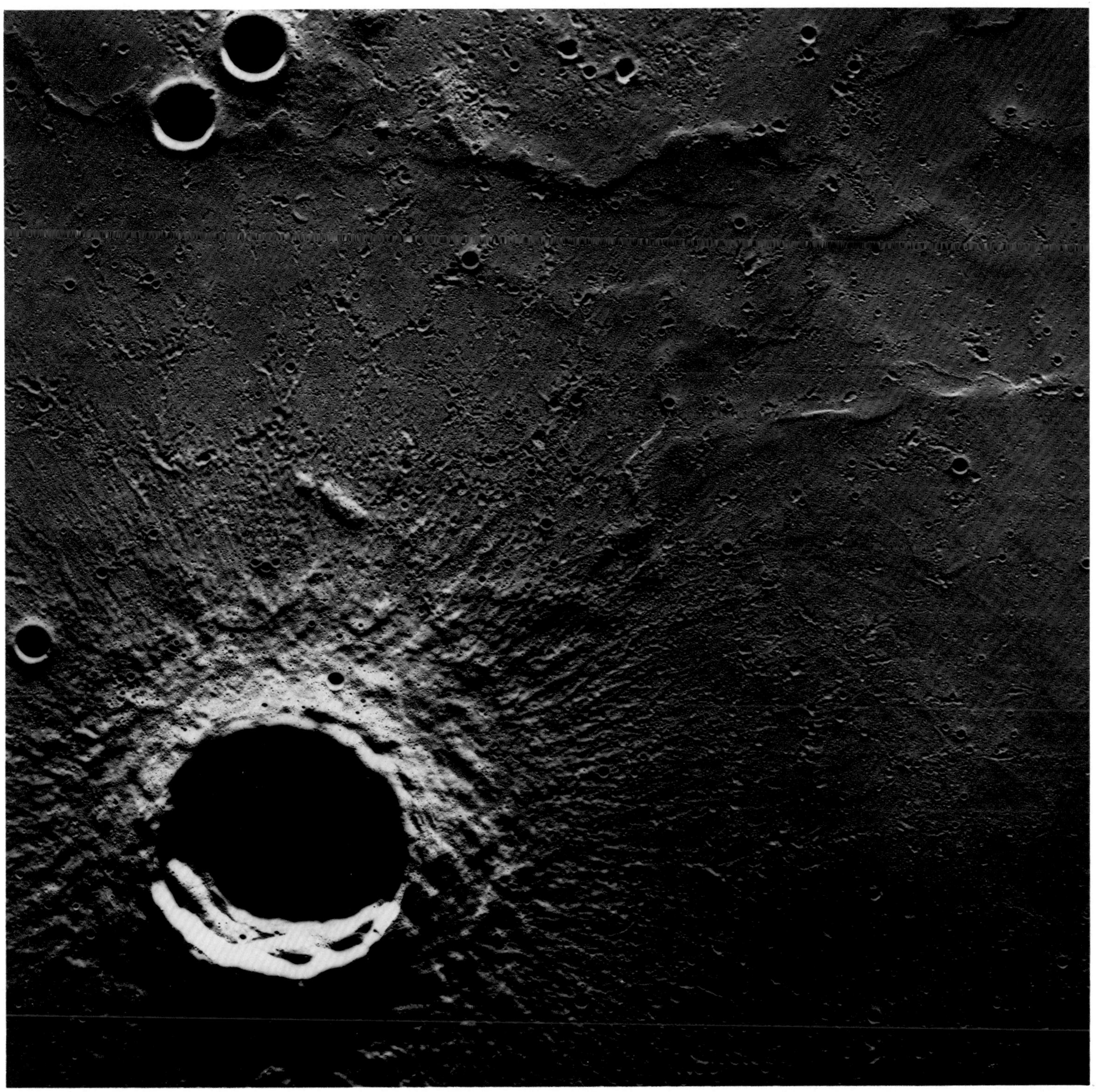

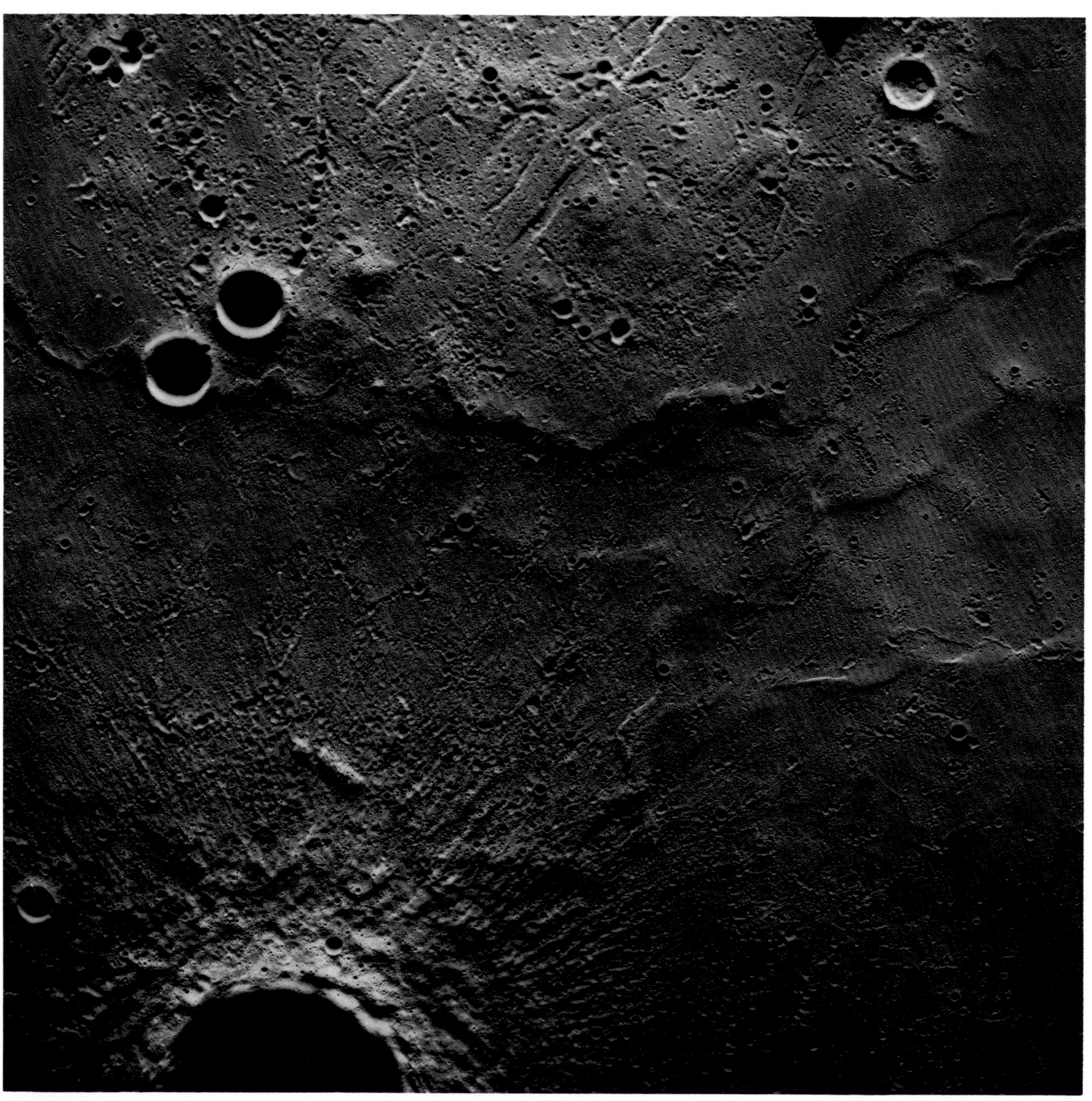

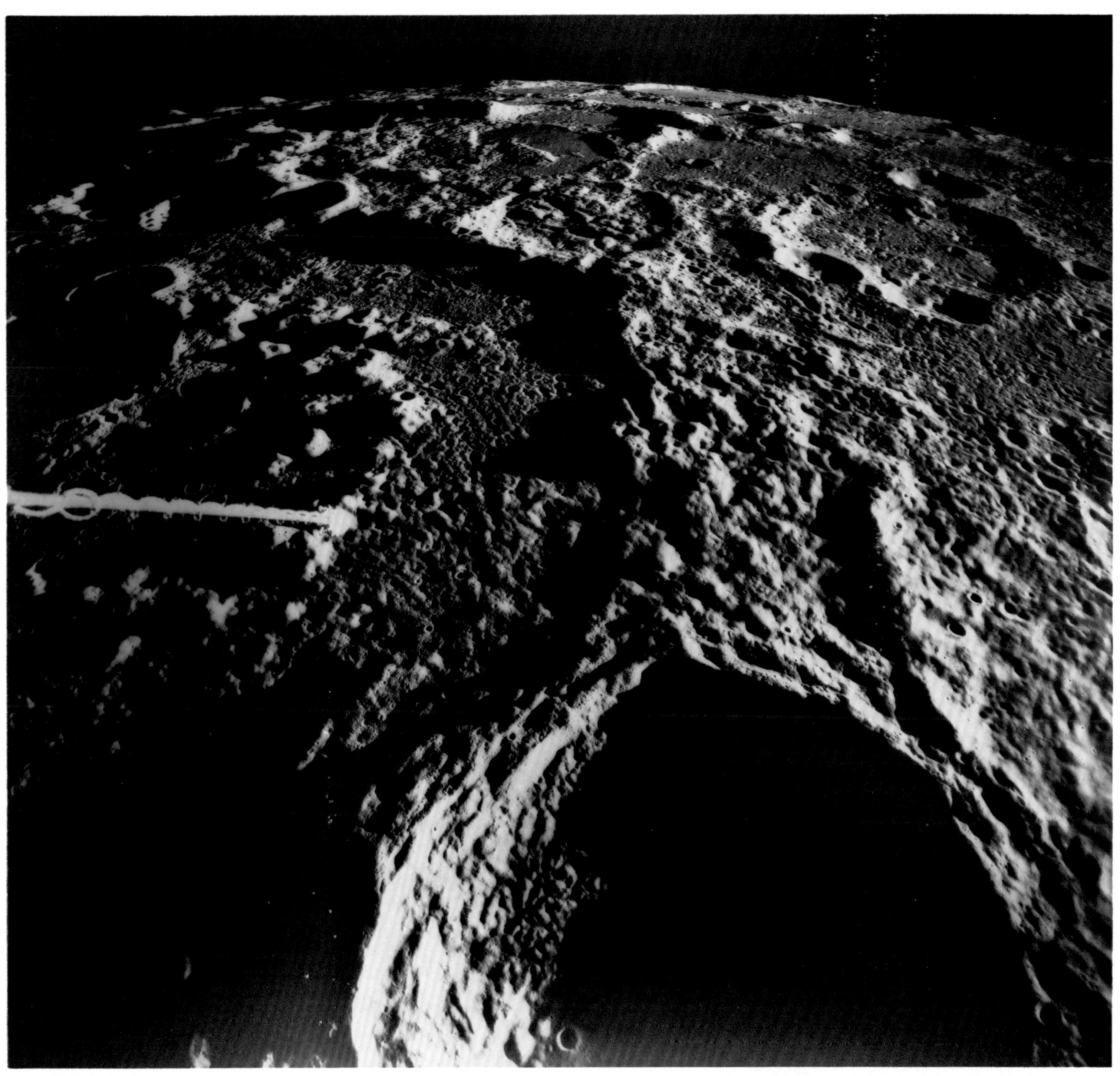

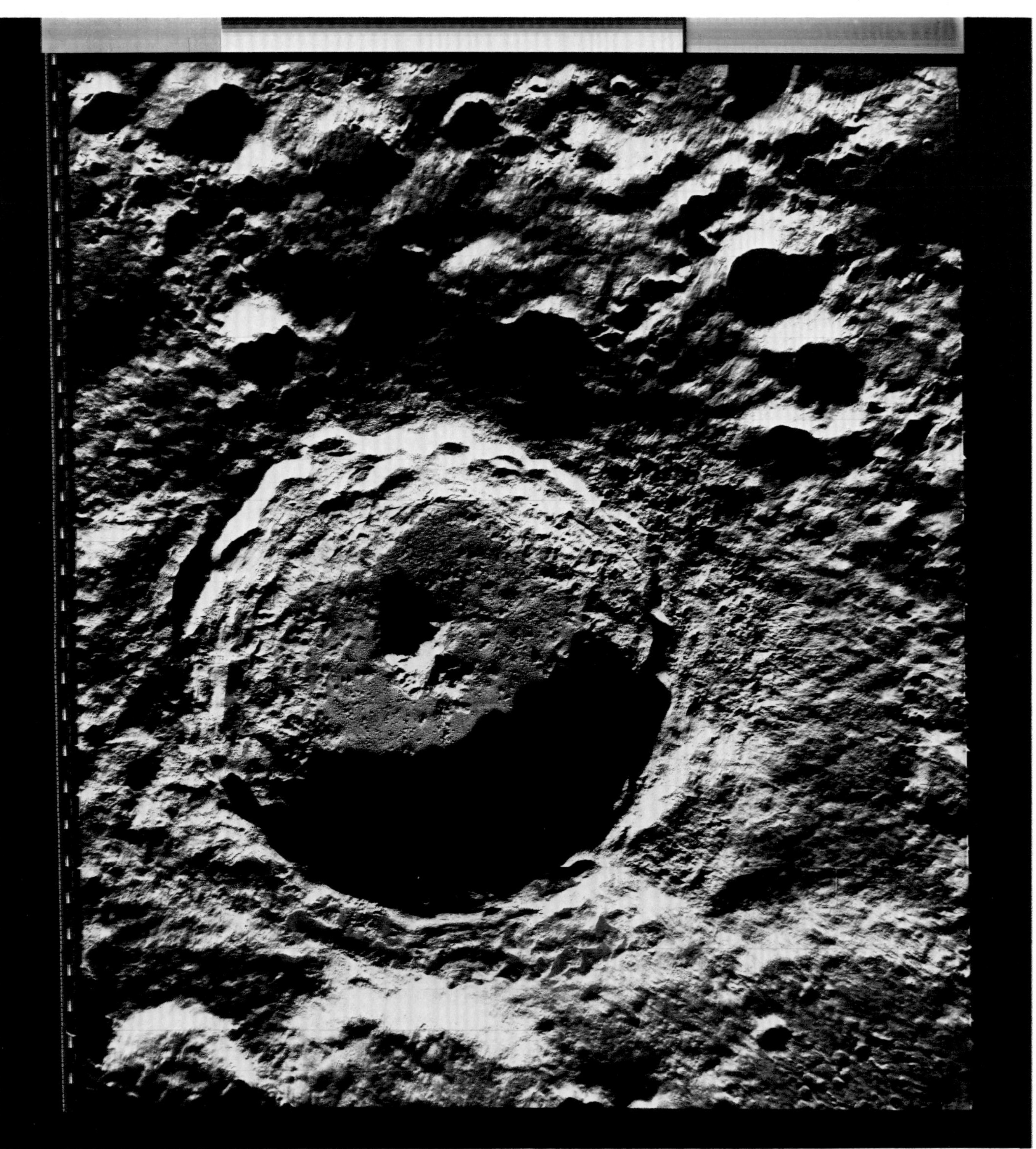

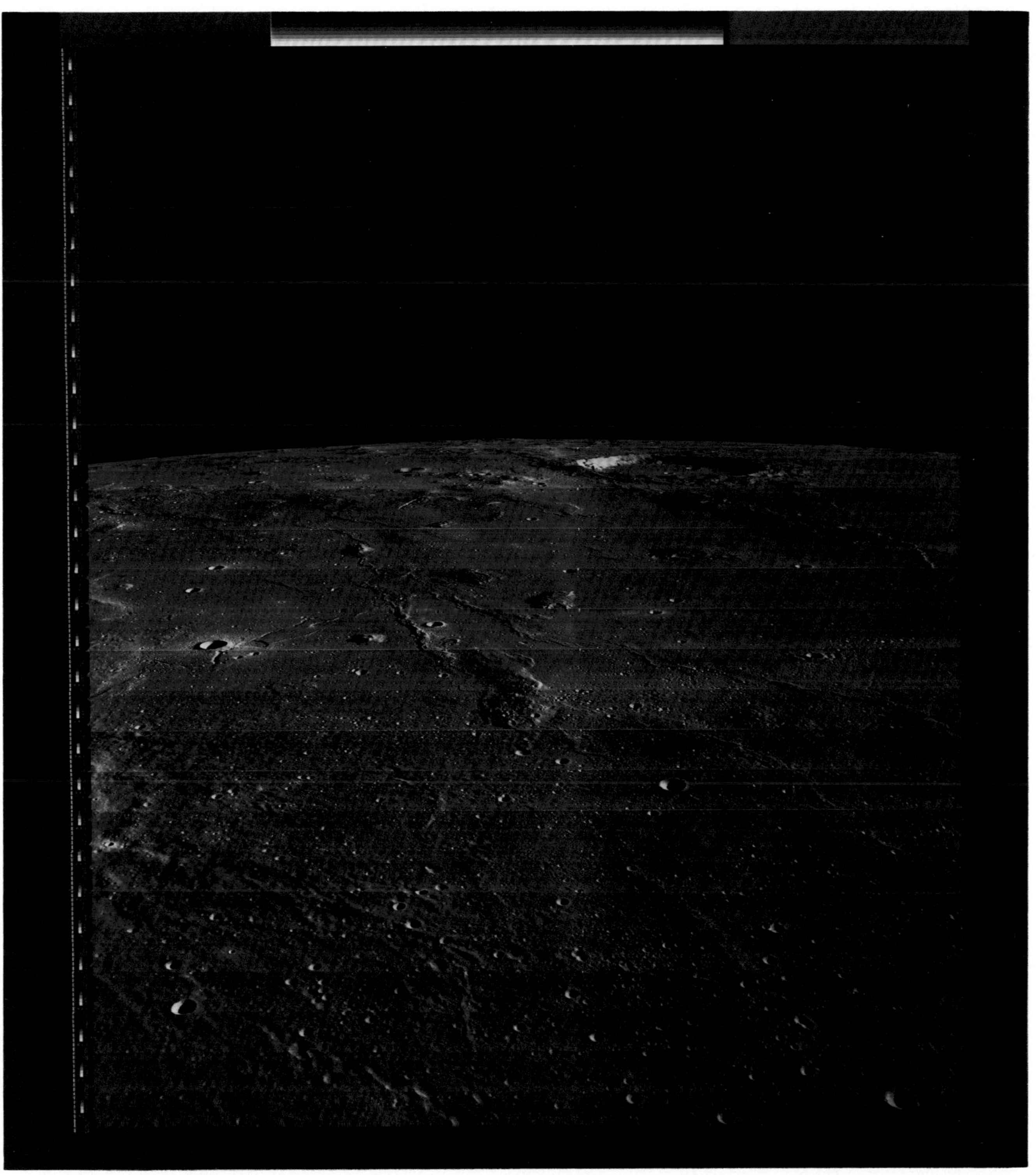

MOON TOPOGRAPHY, CRATER AT TOP, 25 MILES ACROSS

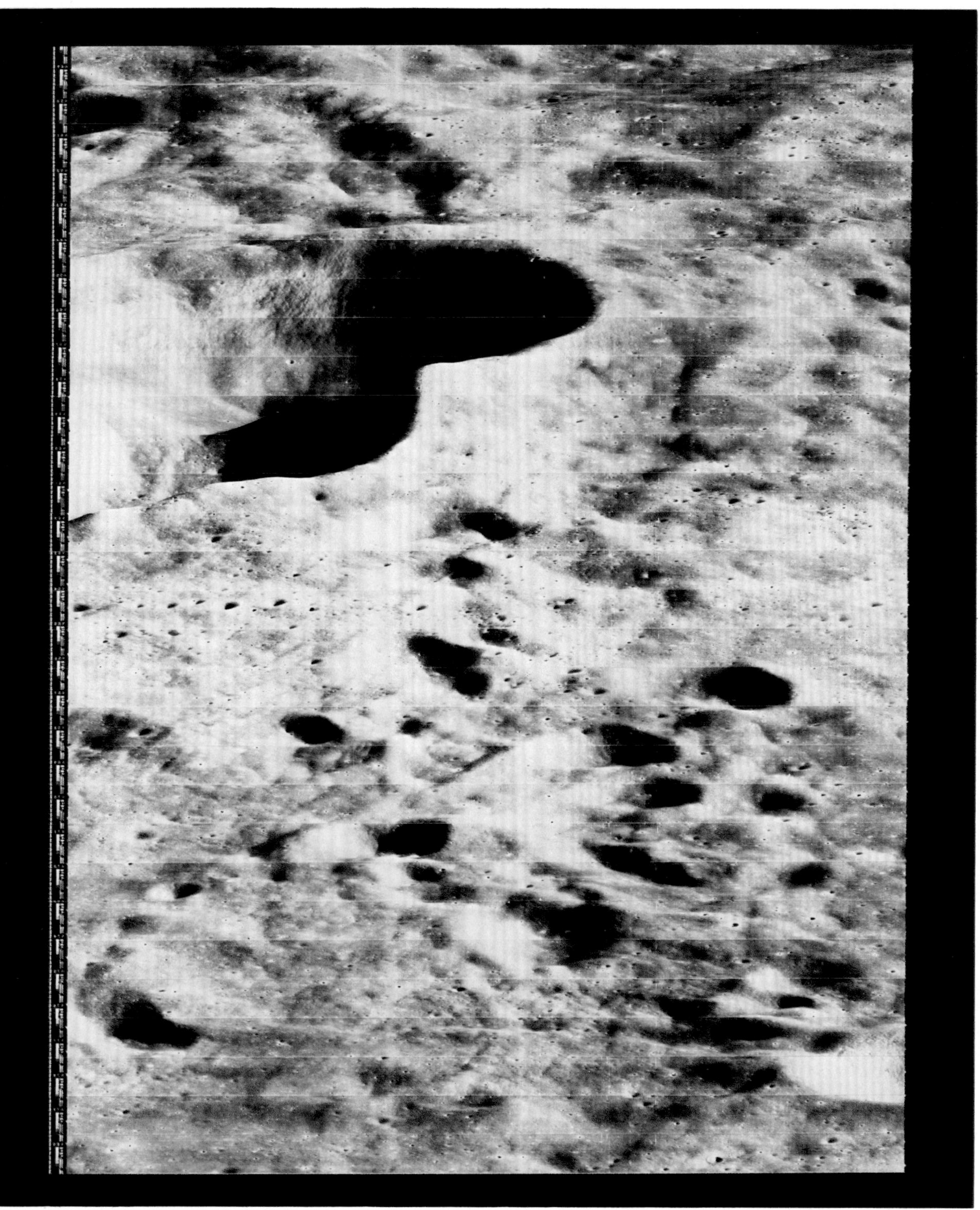

22 LUNAR CRATER

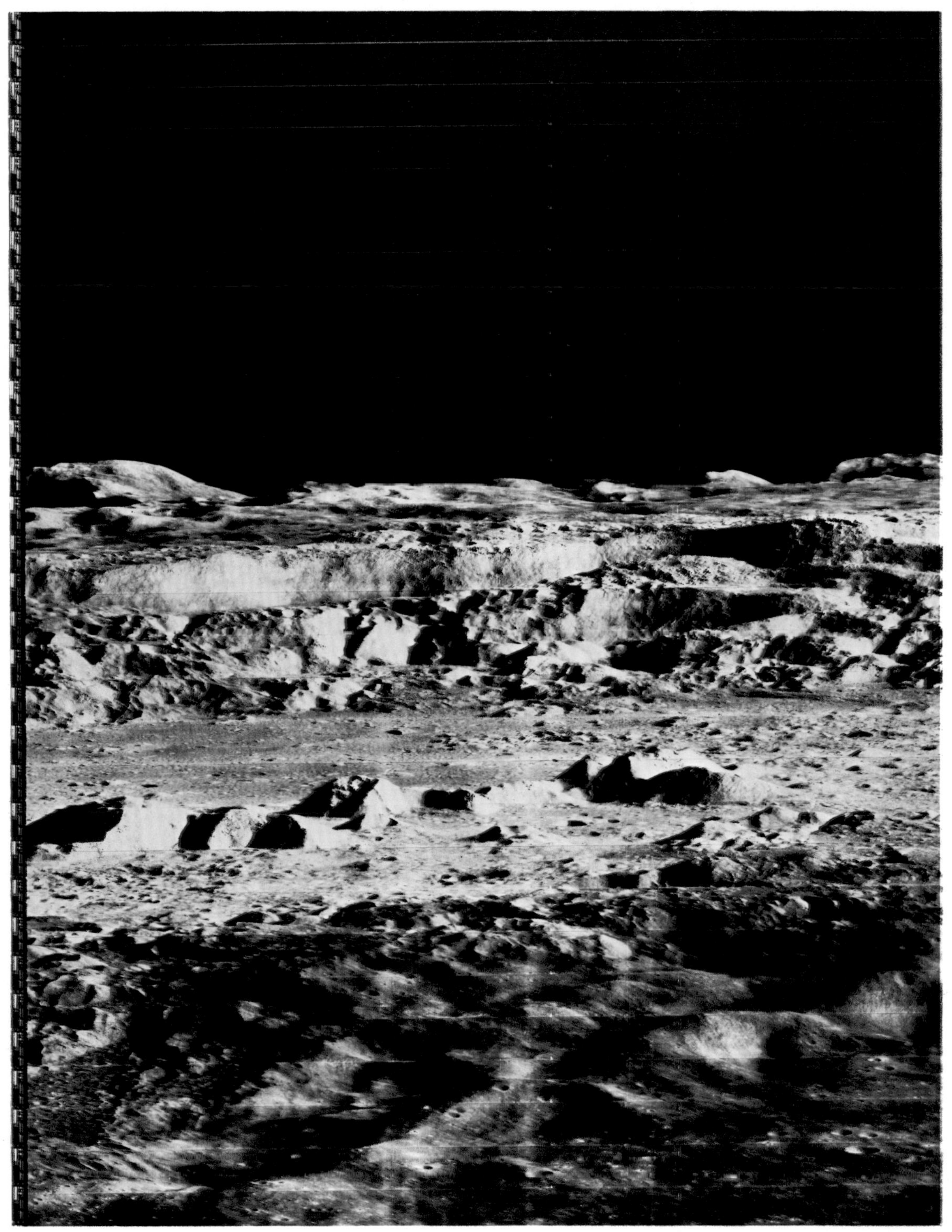

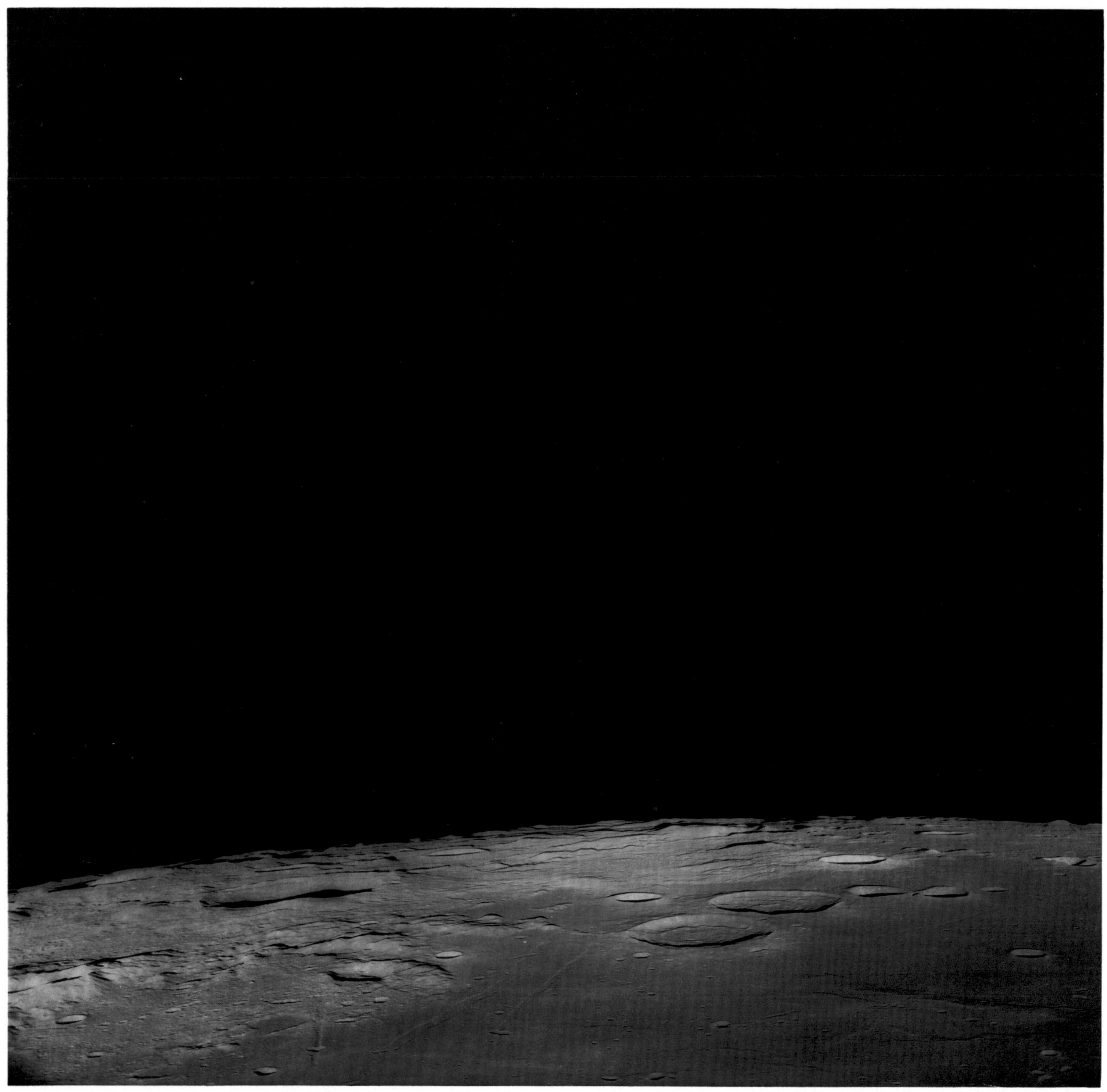

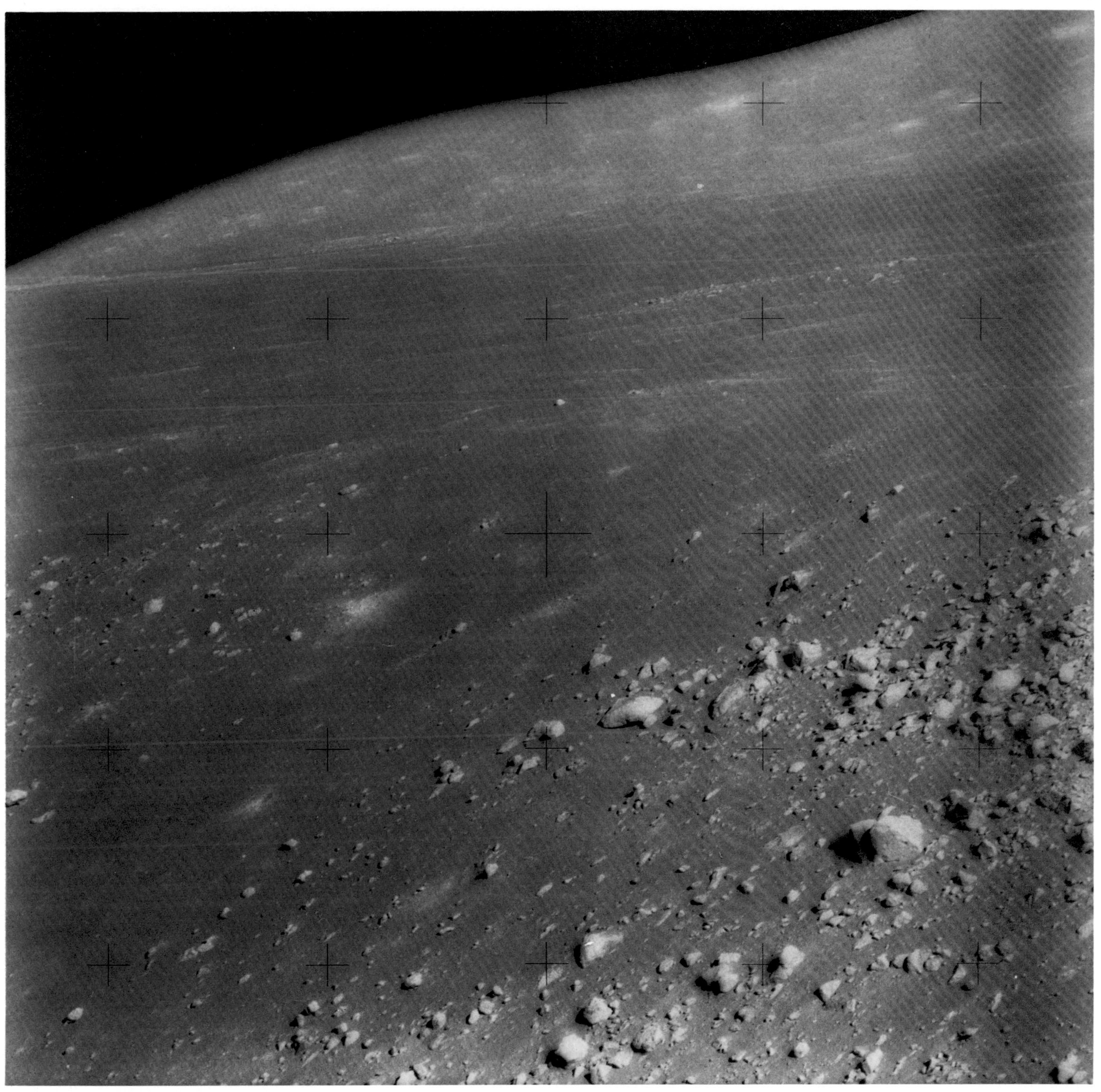

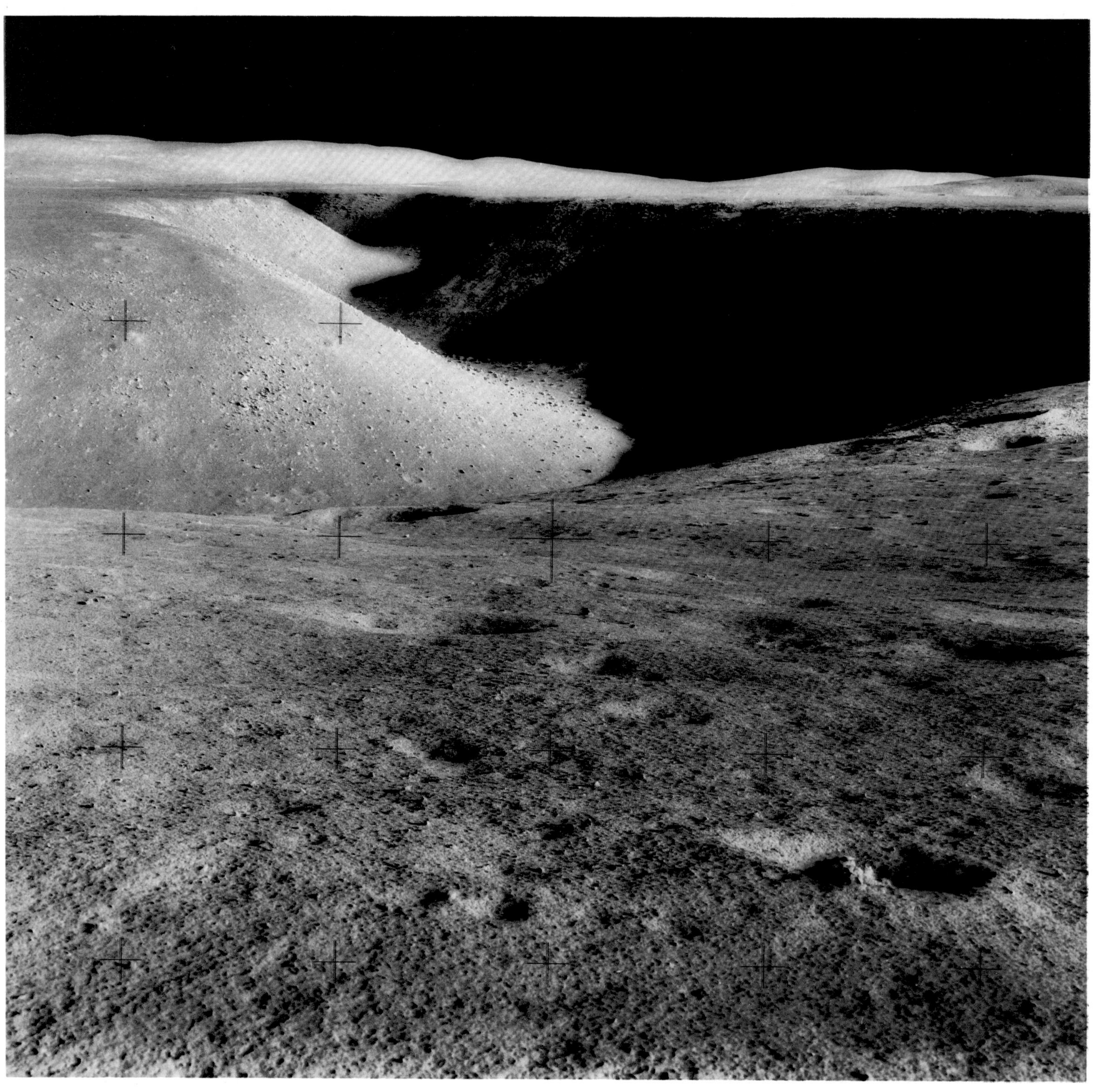

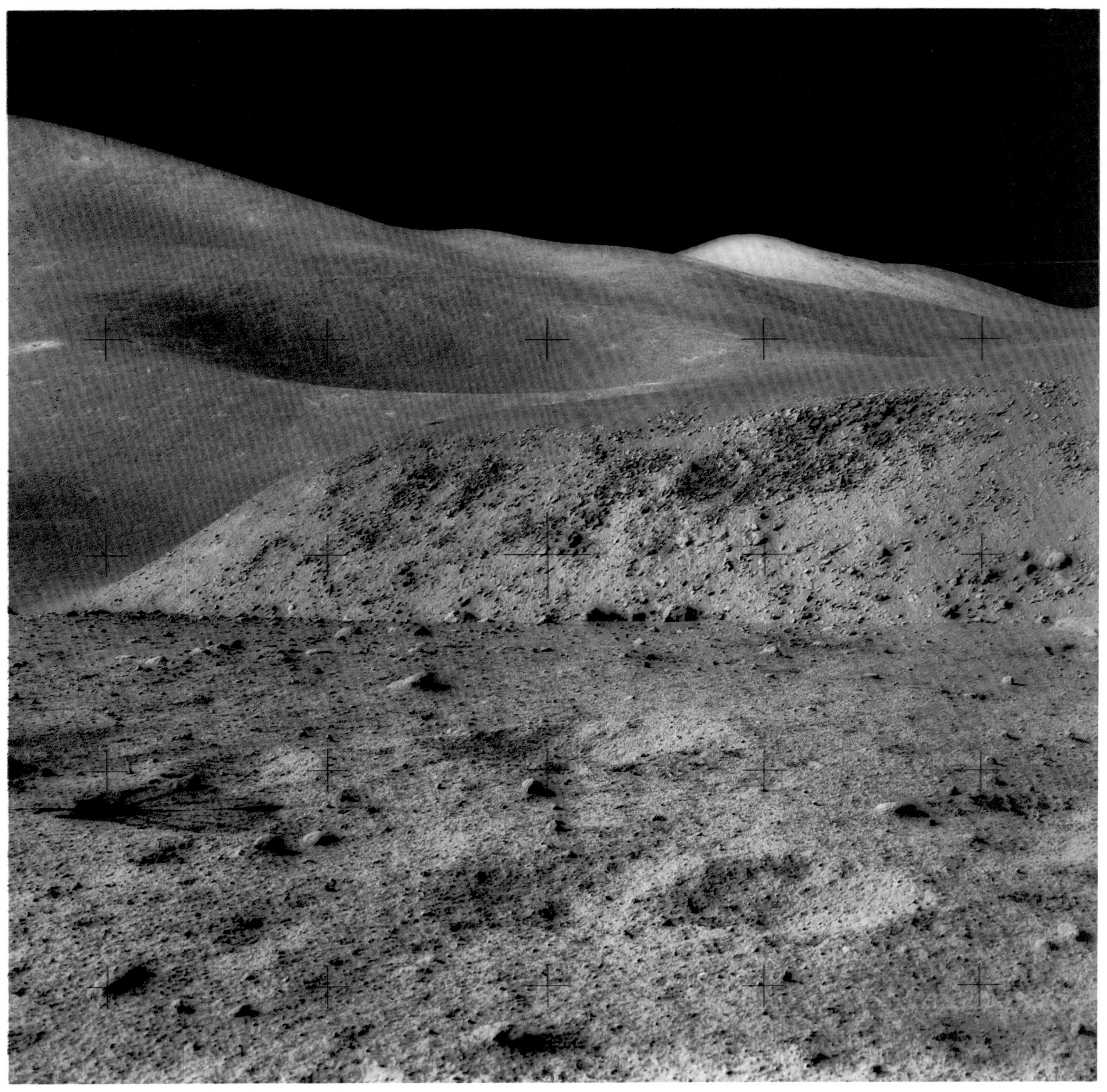

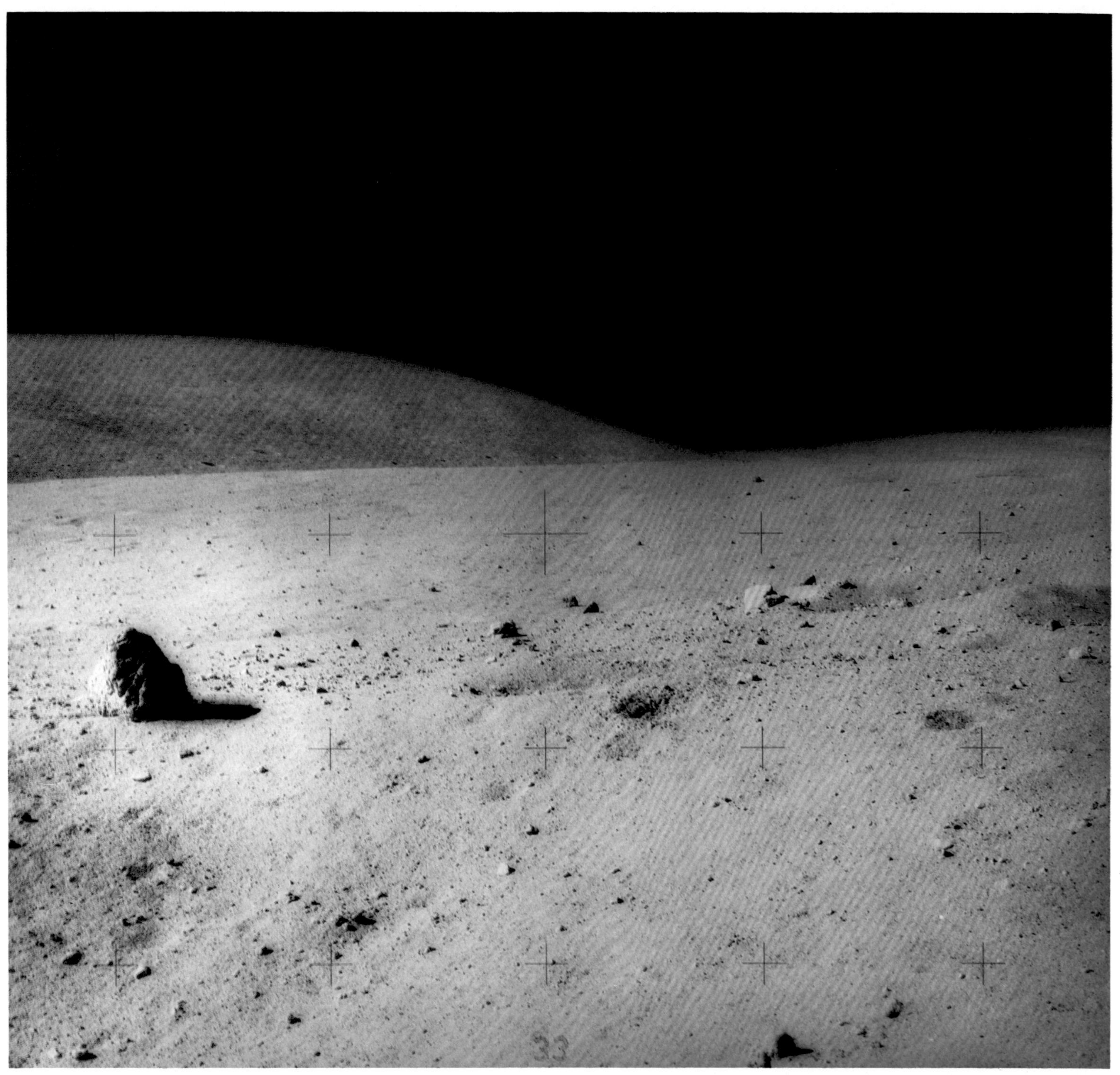

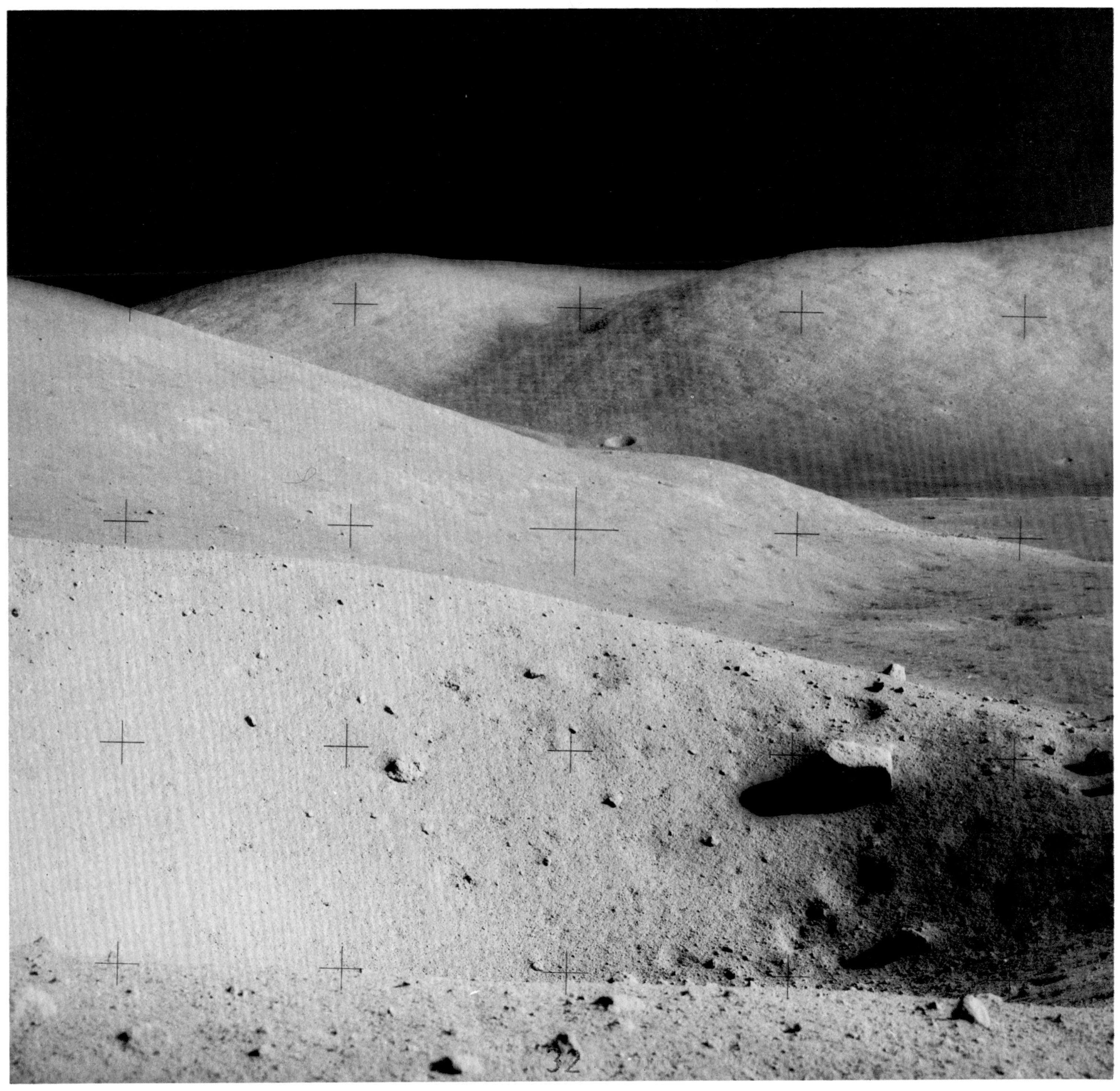

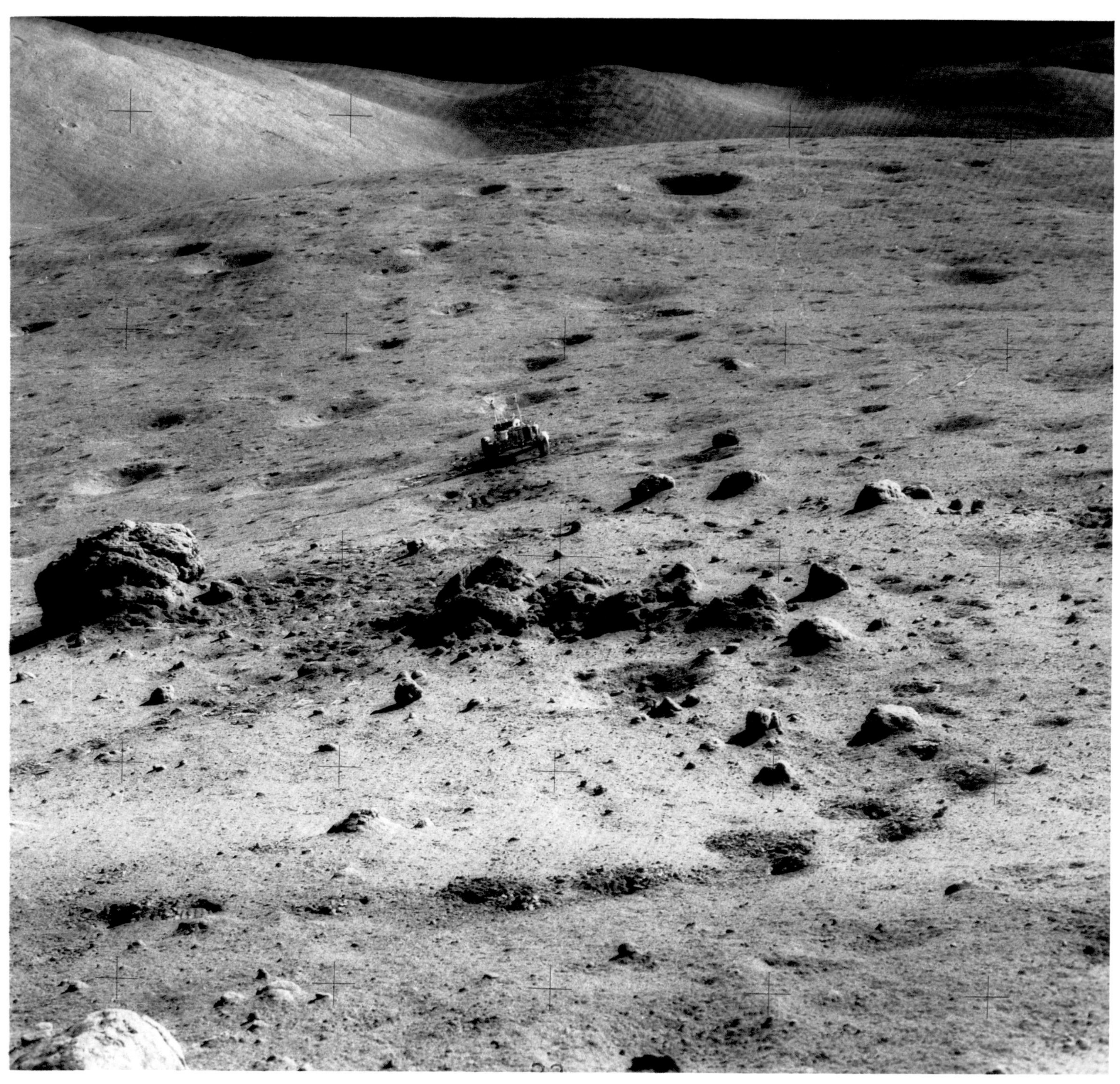

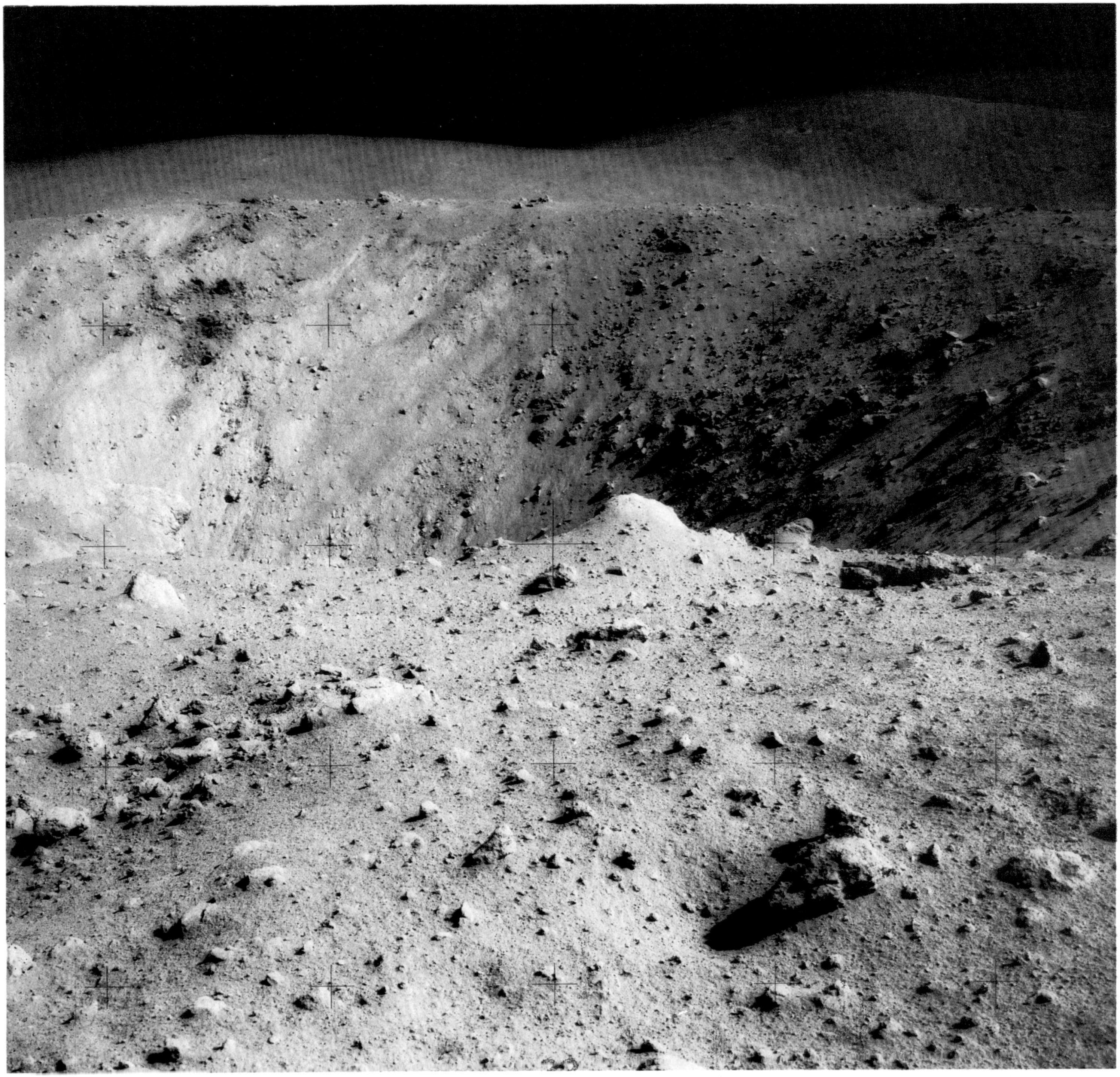

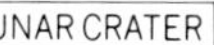

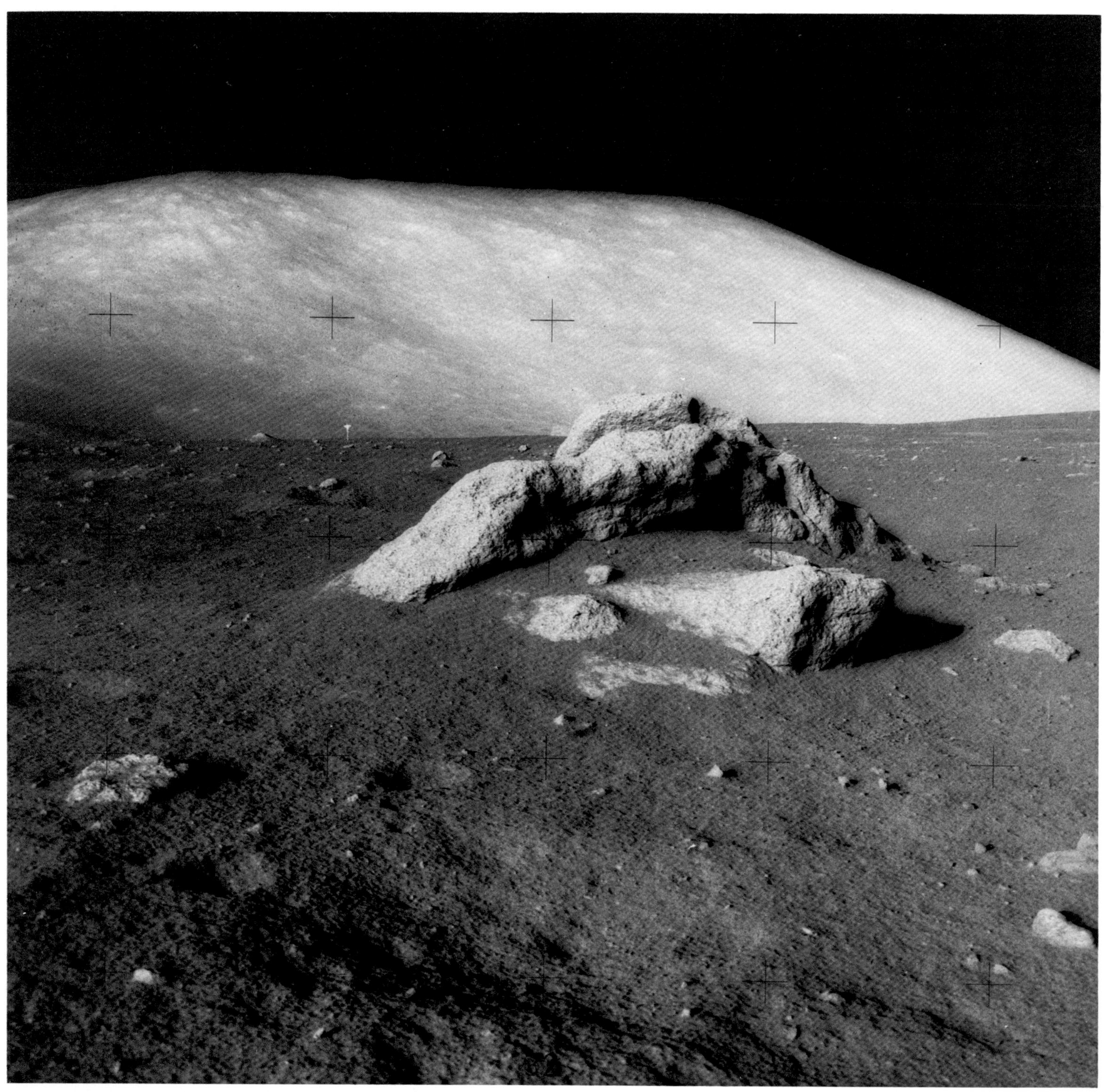

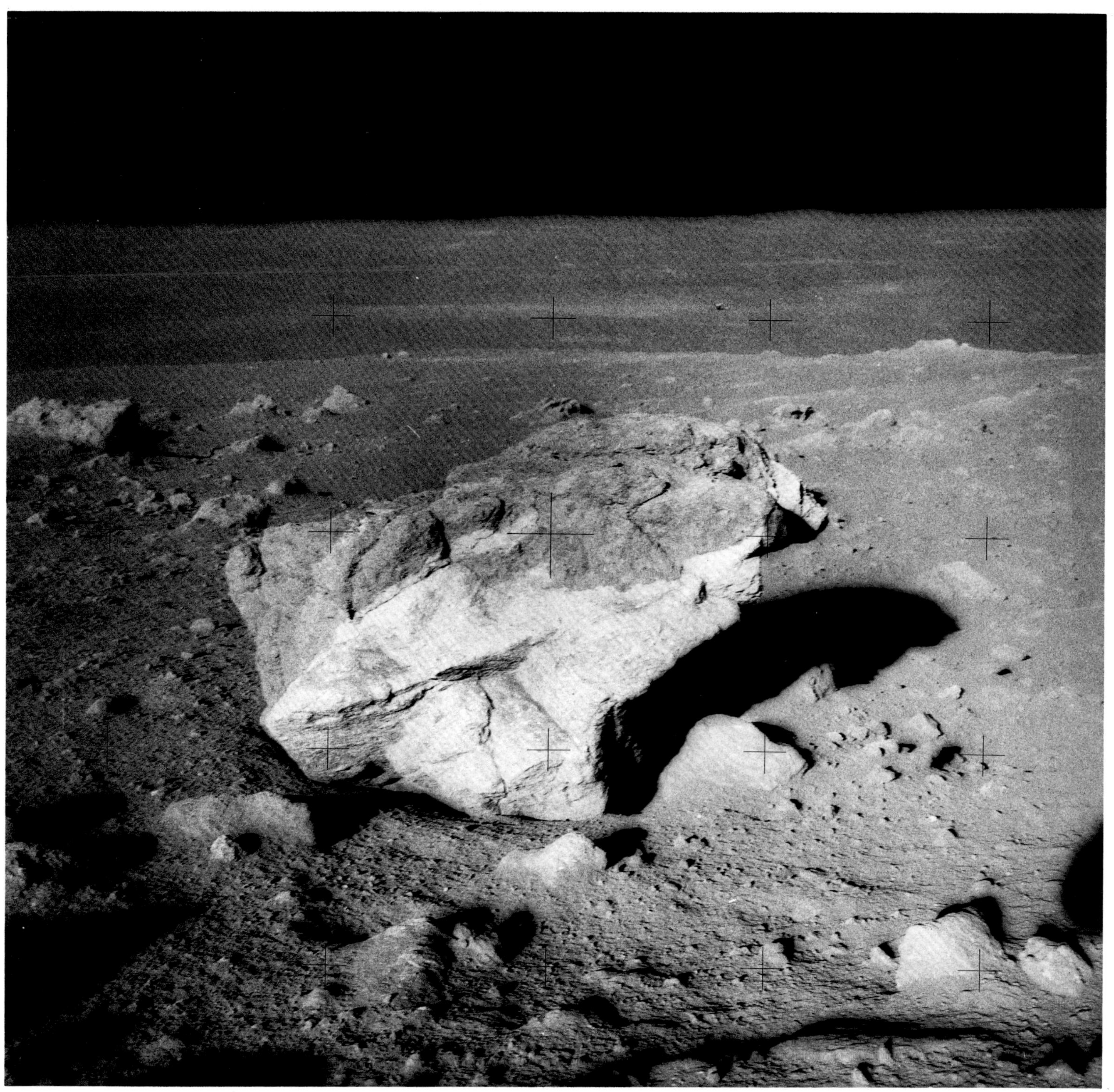

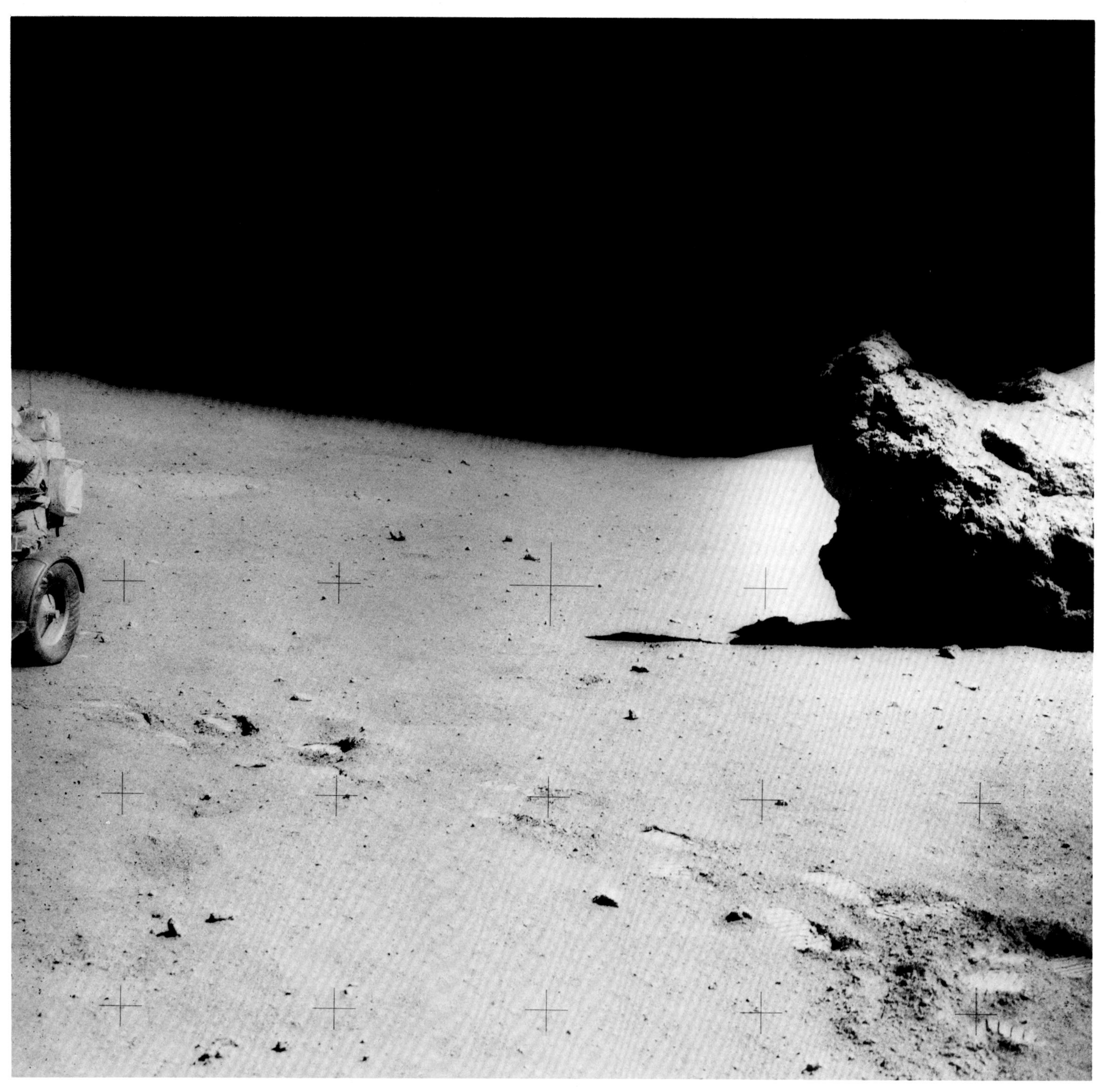

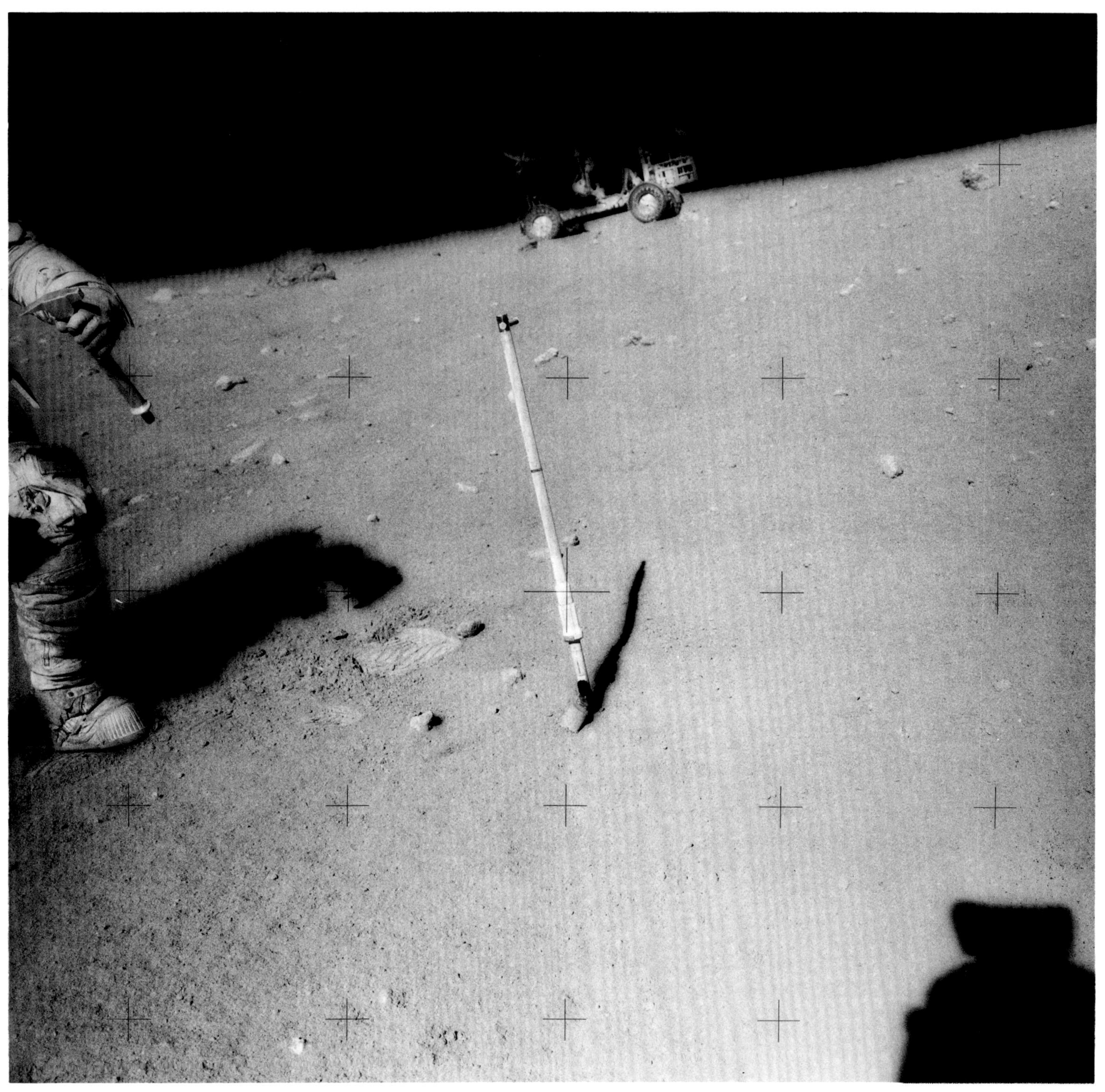

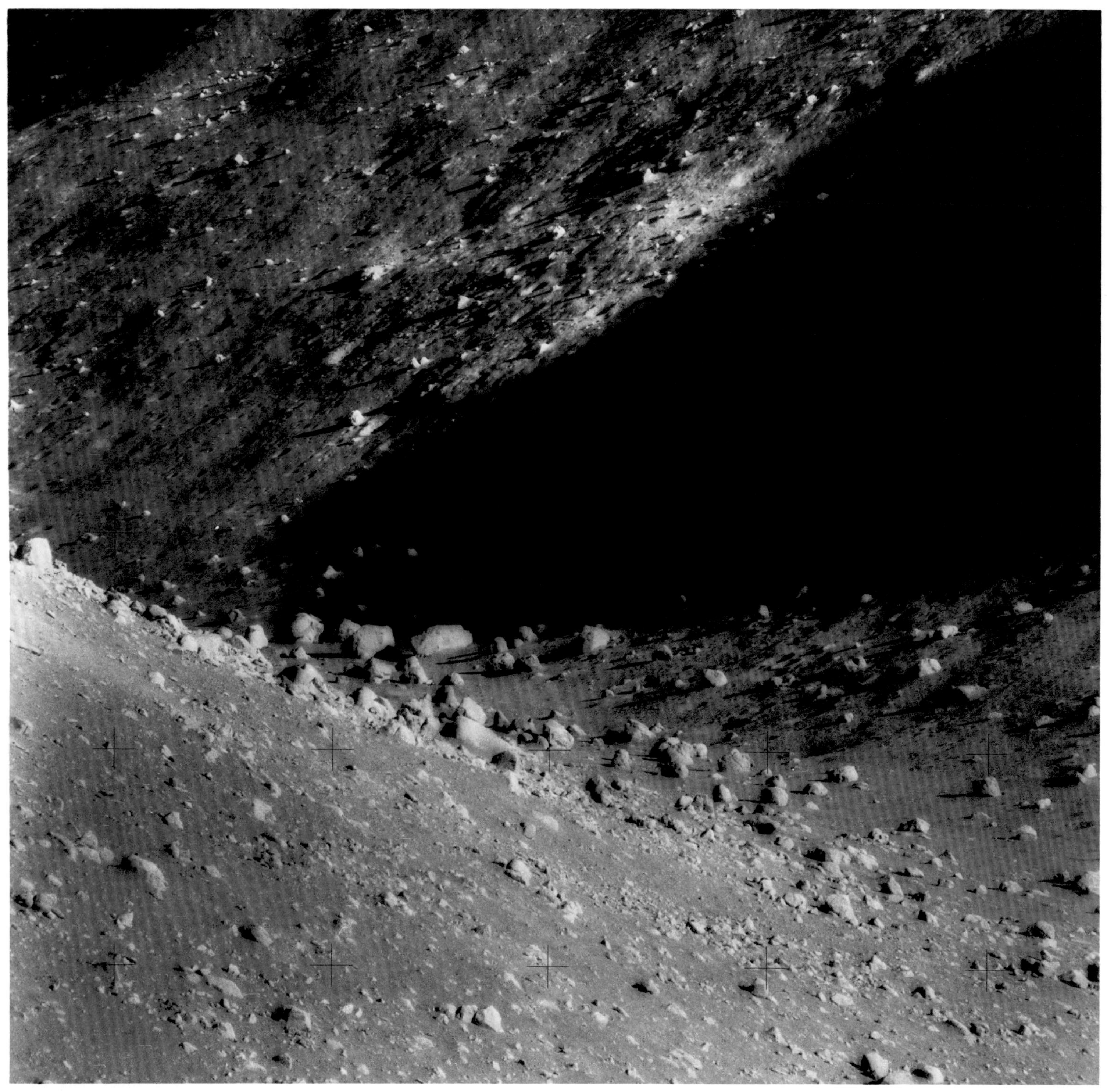

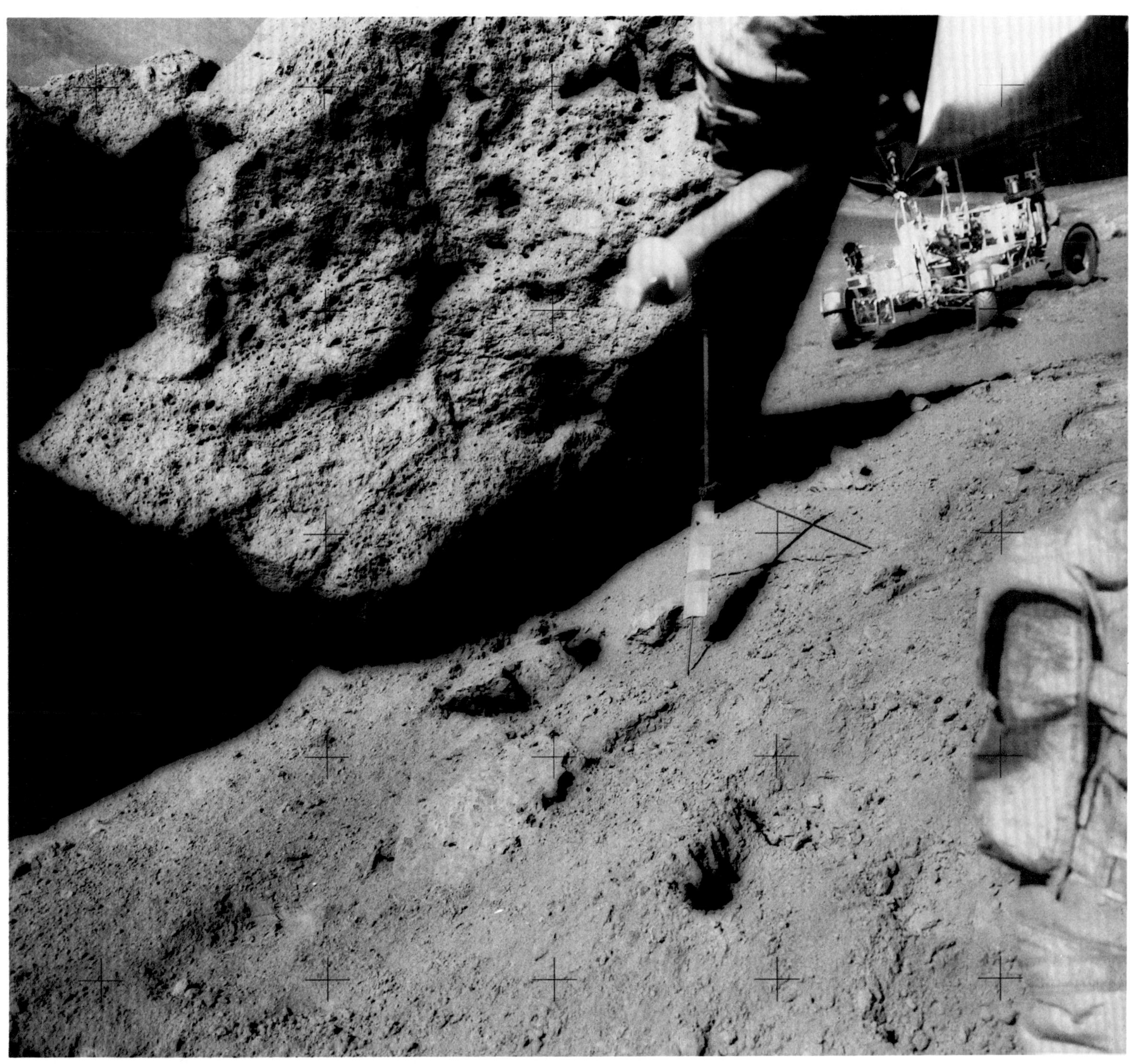

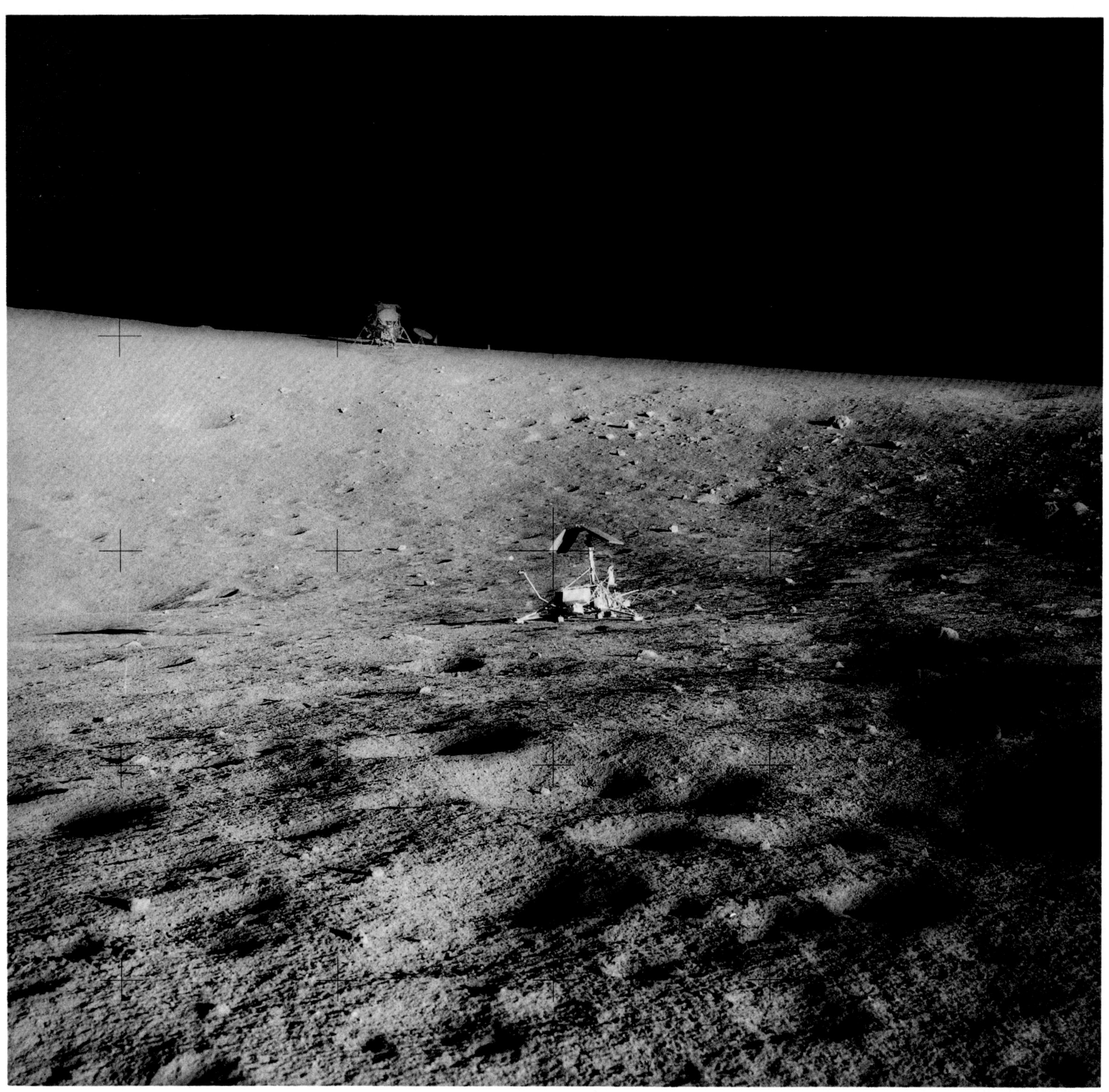

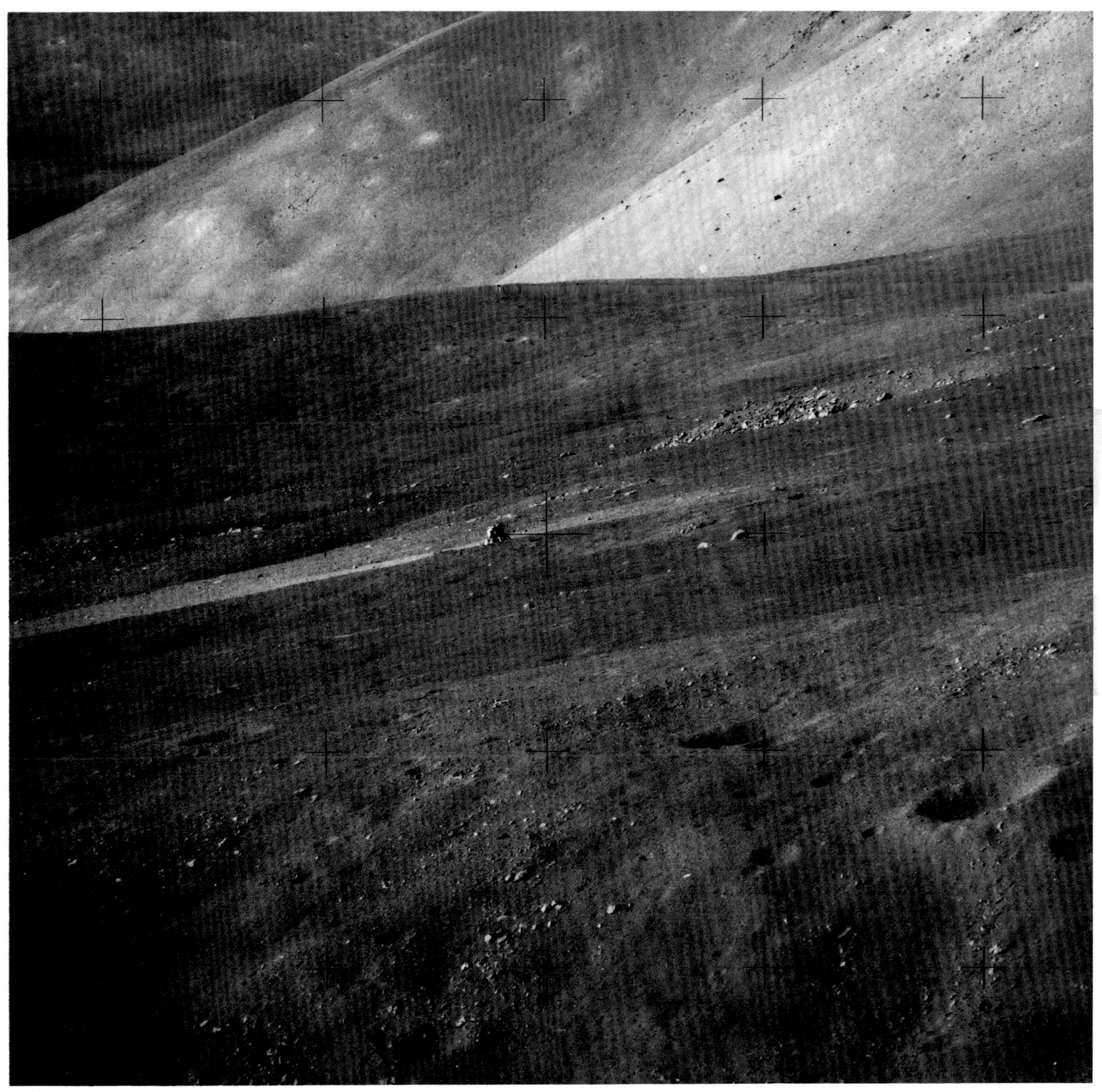

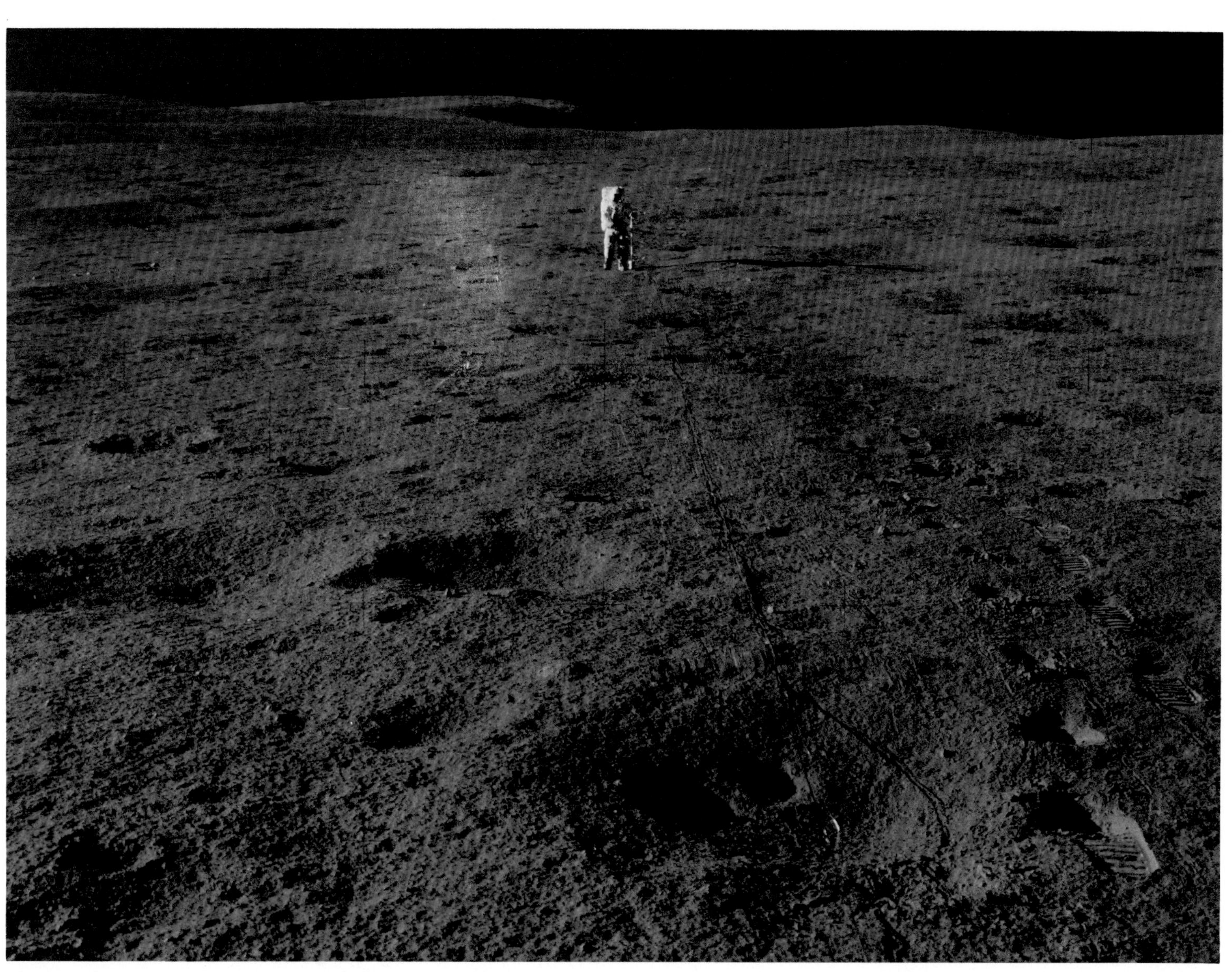

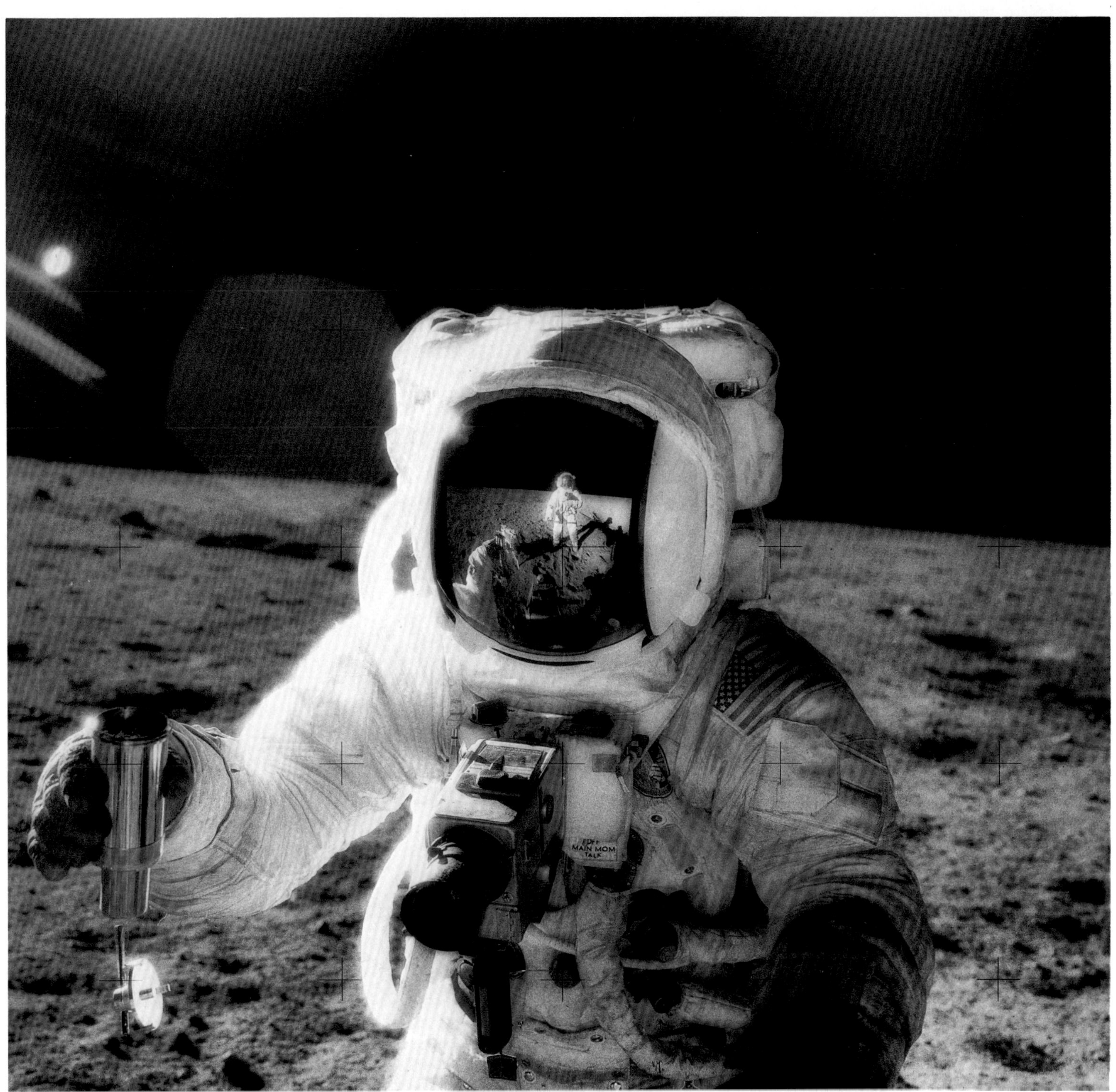

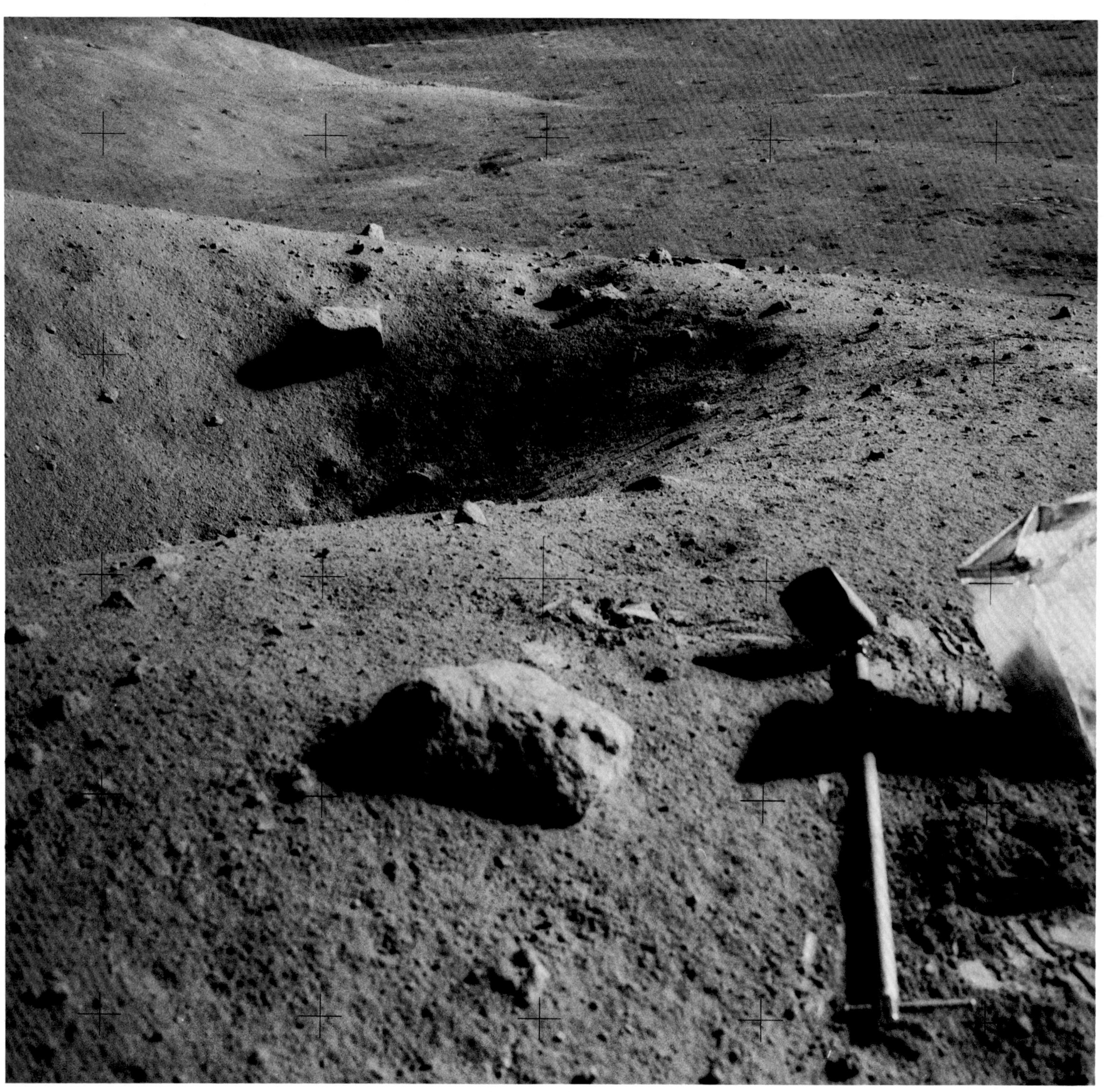

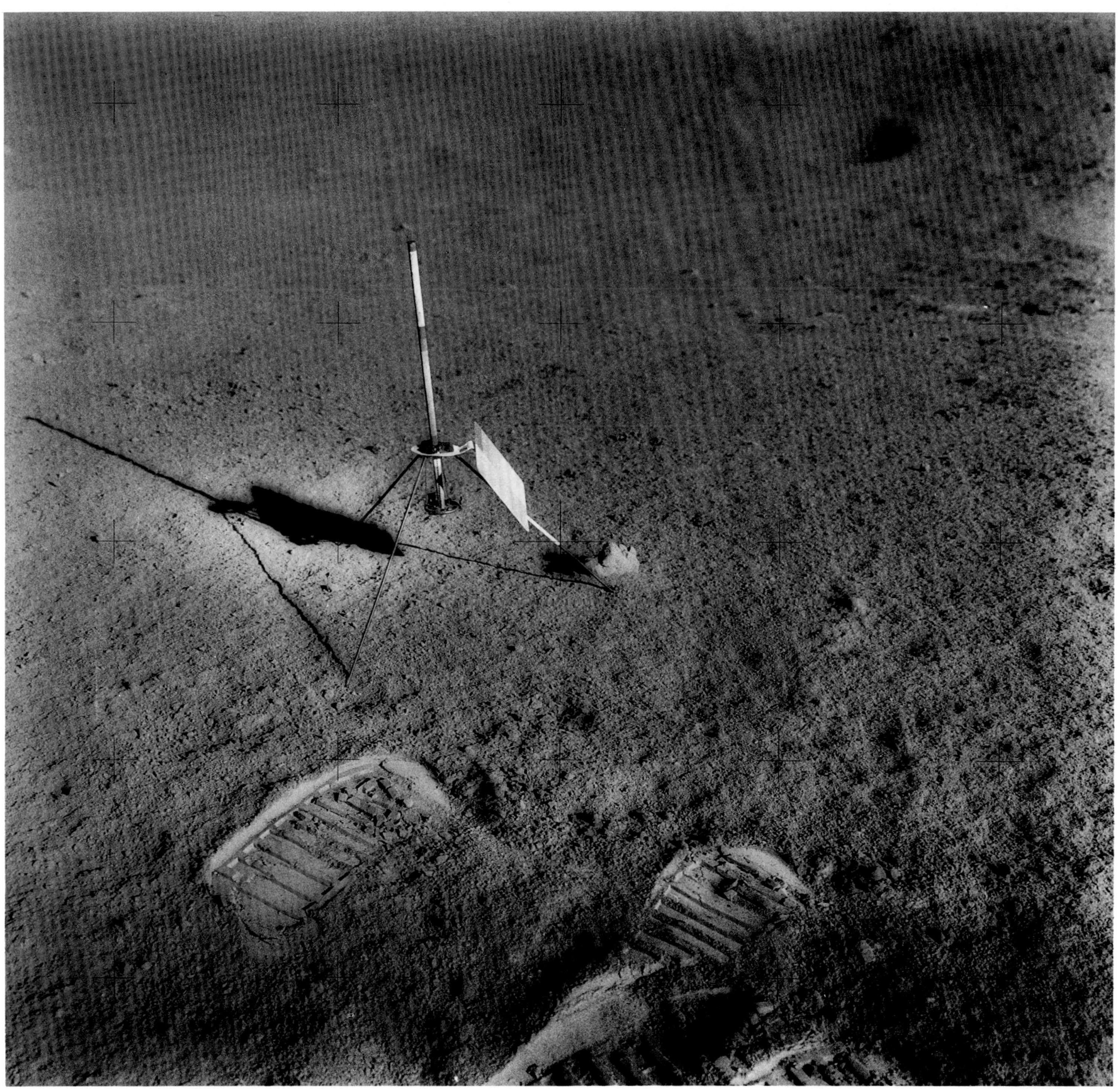

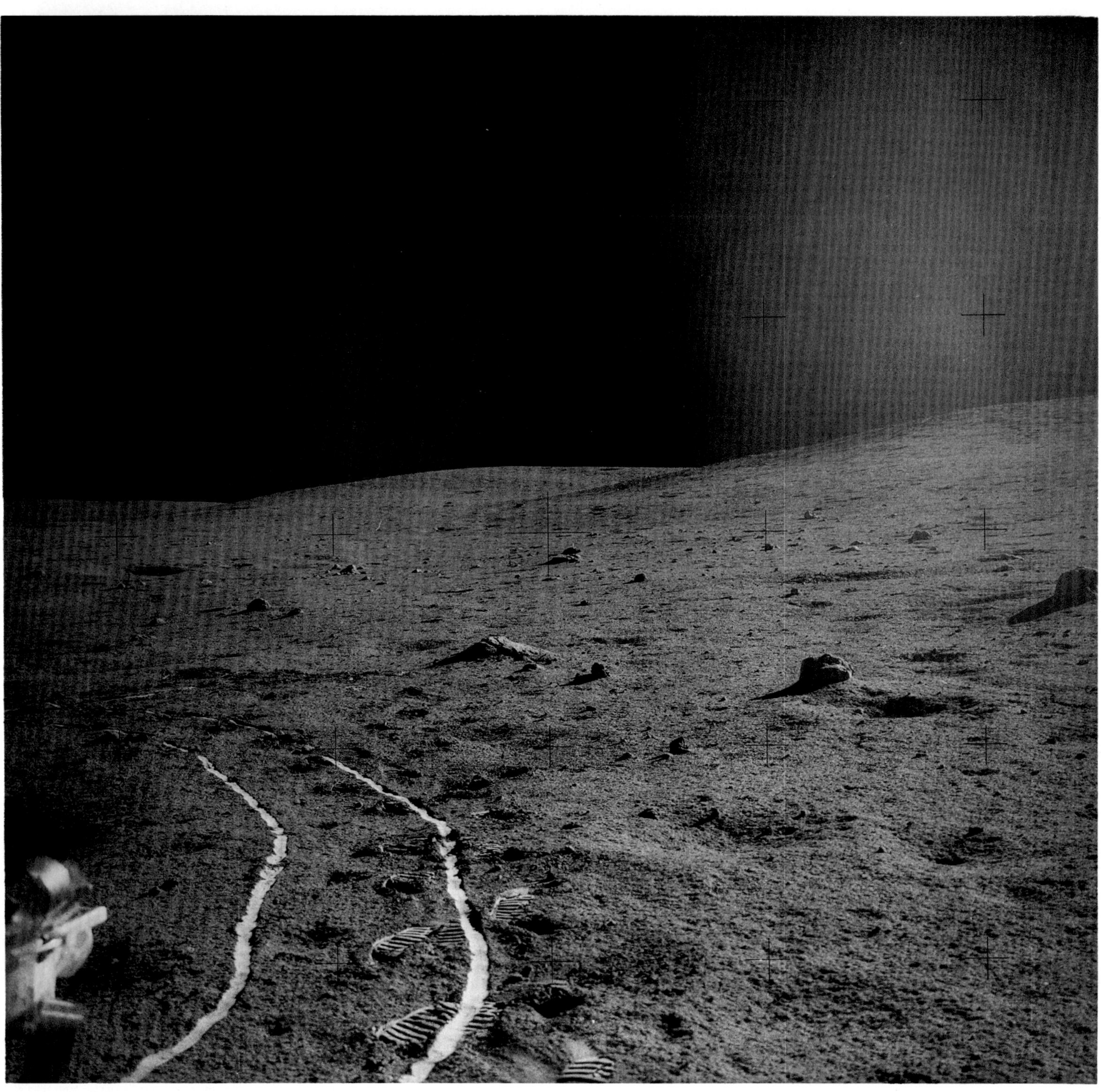

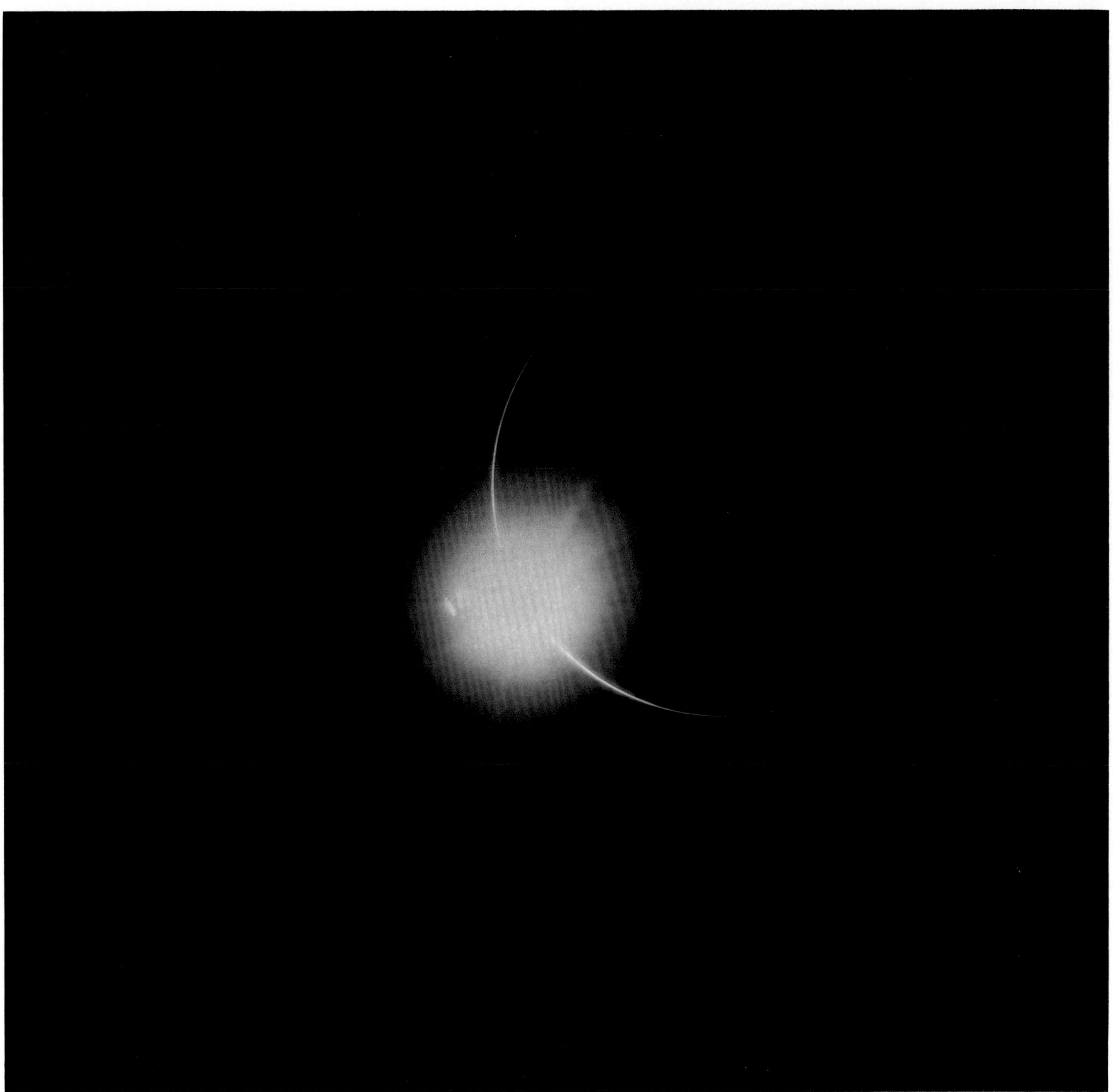

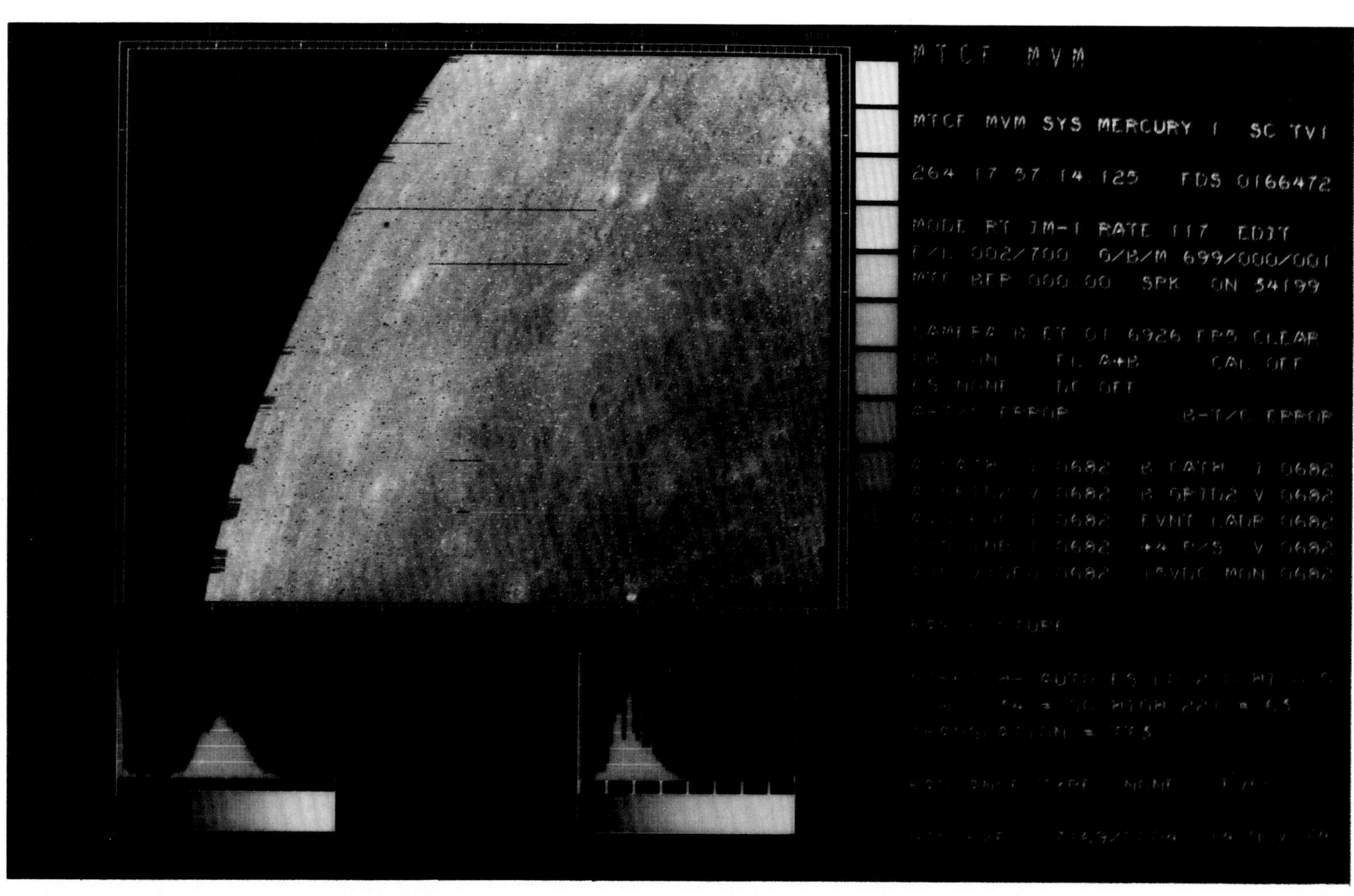
MTCF MVM
MTCF MVM SYS MERCURY I SC TV1
264 17 37 14.125 FDS 0166472
MODE RT IM-1 RATE 117 EDIT
F/L 002/700 G/B/M 699/000/001
SPK ON 34199
B CATH I 0682
B GRID2 V 0682

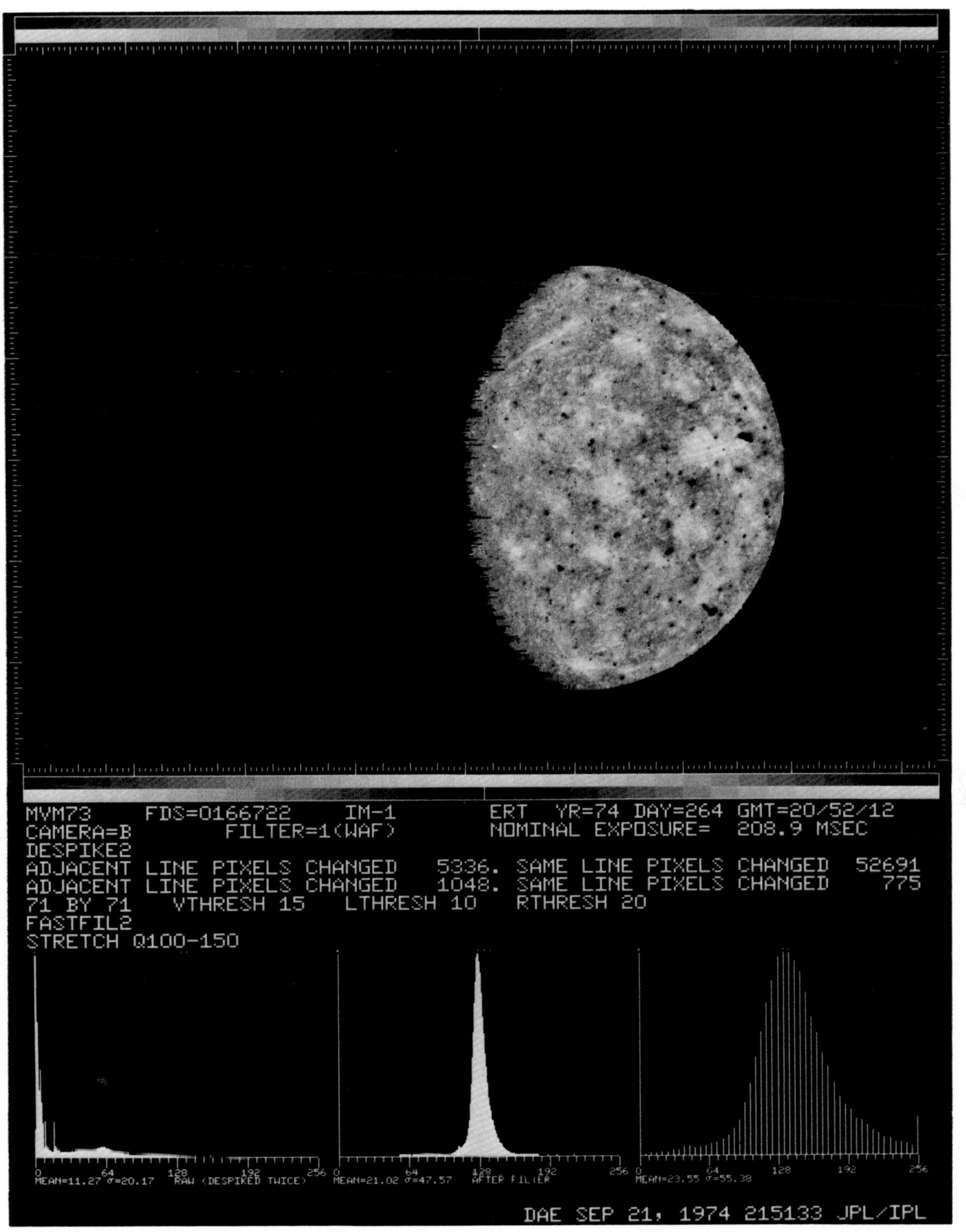
MVM73 FDS=0166722 IM-1 ERT YR=74 DAY=264 GMT=20/52/12
CAMERA=B FILTER=1(WAF) NOMINAL EXPOSURE= 208.9 MSEC
DESPIKE2
ADJACENT LINE PIXELS CHANGED 5336. SAME LINE PIXELS CHANGED 52691
ADJACENT LINE PIXELS CHANGED 1048. SAME LINE PIXELS CHANGED 775
71 BY 71 VTHRESH 15 LTHRESH 10 RTHRESH 20
FASTFIL2
STRETCH Q100-150
0 64 128 192 256
MEAN=11.27 σ=20.17 RAW (DESPIKED TWICE)
0 64 128 192 256
MEAN=21.02 σ=47.57 AFTER FILTER
0 64 128 192 256
MEAN=23.55 σ=55.38
DAE SEP 21, 1974 215133 JPL/IPL

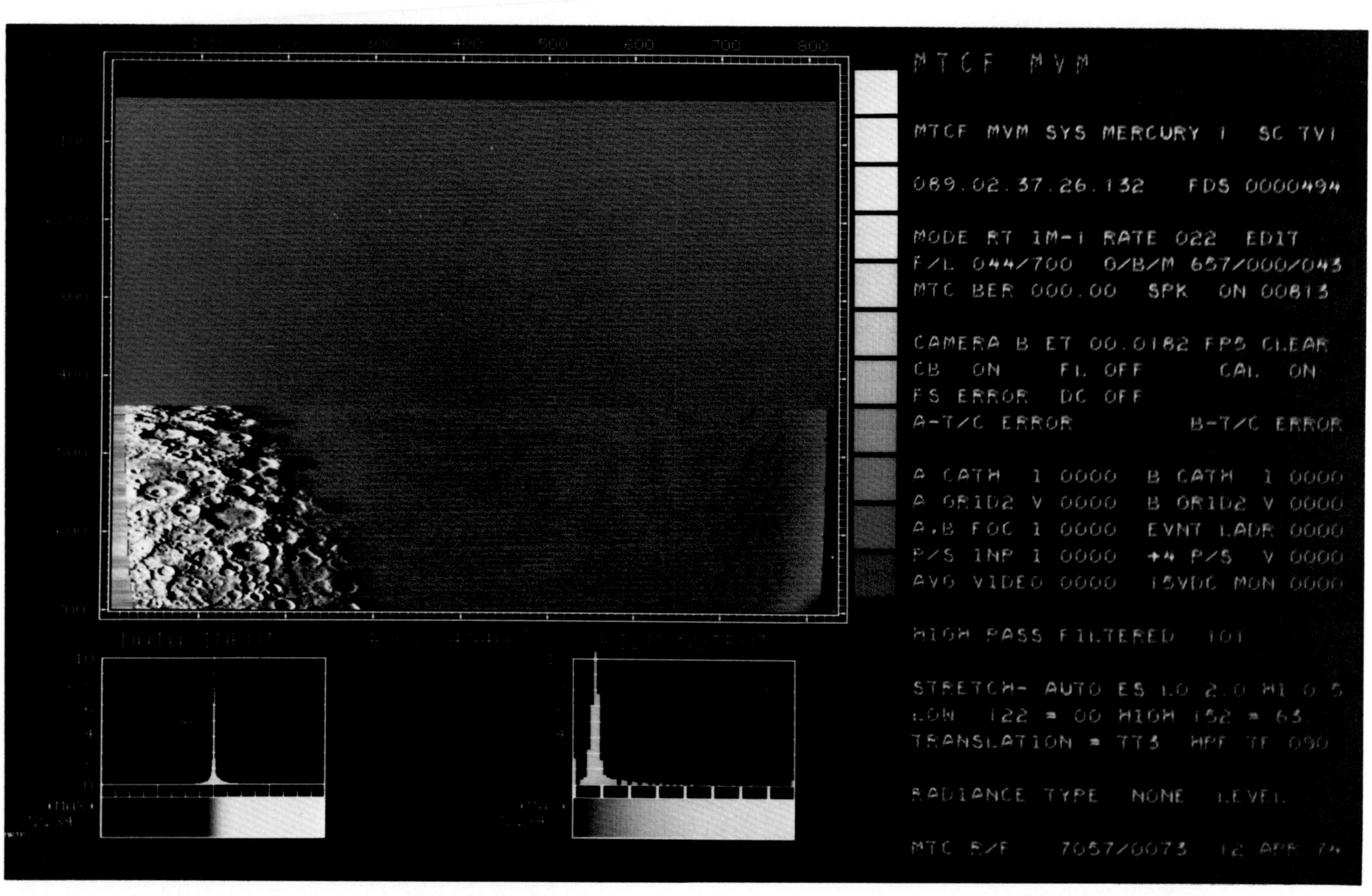
MTCF MVM
MTCF MVM SYS MERCURY 1 SC TV1
089.02.37.26.132 FDS 0000494
MODE RT IM-1 RATE 022 EDIT
F/L 044/700 O/B/M 657/000/043
MTC BER 000.00 SPK ON 00813
CAMERA B ET 00.0182 FPS CLEAR
CB ON FL OFF CAL ON
FS ERROR DC OFF
A-T/C ERROR B-T/C ERROR
A CATH I 0000 B CATH I 0000
A GRID2 V 0000 B GRID2 V 0000
A,B FOC I 0000 EVNT LADR 0000
P/S INP I 0000 +4 P/S V 0000
AVG VIDEO 0000 15VDC MON 0000
HIGH PASS FILTERED 101
STRETCH- AUTO ES LO 2.0 HI 0.5
LOW 122 = 00 HIGH 152 = 63
TRANSLATION = TT3 HPF TF 090
RADIANCE TYPE NONE LEVEL
MTC R/F 7057/0073 12 APR 74

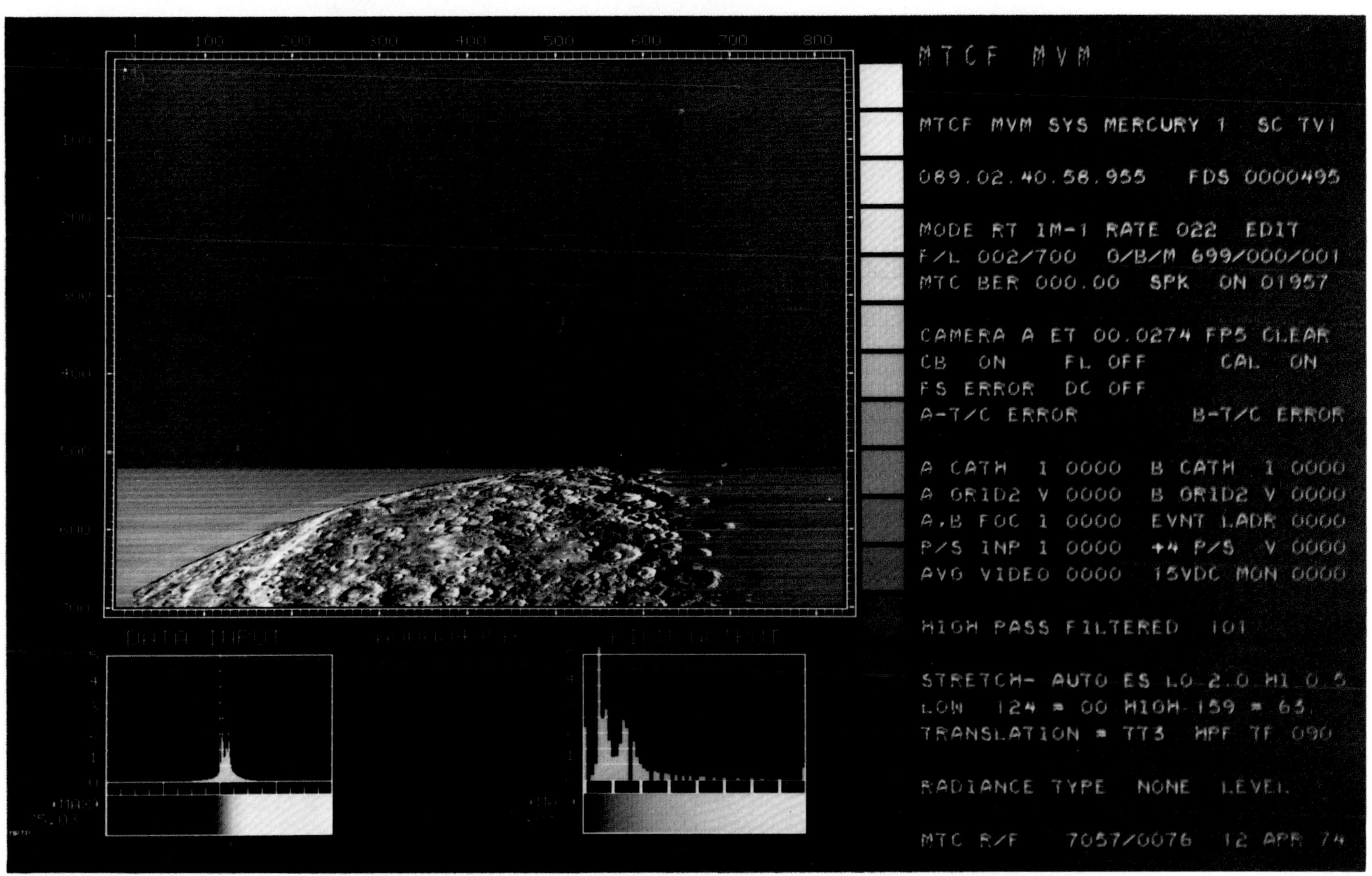

1 100 200 300 400 500 600 700 800
MTCF MVM
MTCF MVM SYS MERCURY 1 SC TV1
089.02.40.58.955 FDS 0000495
MODE RT 1M-1 RATE 022 EDIT
F/L 002/700 0/B/M 699/000/001
MTC BER 000.00 SPK ON 01957
CAMERA A ET 00.0274 FPS CLEAR
CB ON FL OFF CAL ON
FS ERROR DC OFF
A-T/C ERROR B-T/C ERROR
A CATH I 0000 B CATH I 0000
A GRID2 V 0000 B GRID2 V 0000
A,B FOC I 0000 EVNT LADR 0000
P/S INP I 0000 +4 P/S V 0000
AVG VIDEO 0000 15VDC MON 0000
HIGH PASS FILTERED 101
STRETCH- AUTO ES LO 2.0 HI 0.5
LOW 124 = 00 HIGH 159 = 63.
TRANSLATION = 773 HPF TF 090
RADIANCE TYPE NONE LEVEL
MTC R/F 7057/0076 12 APR 74

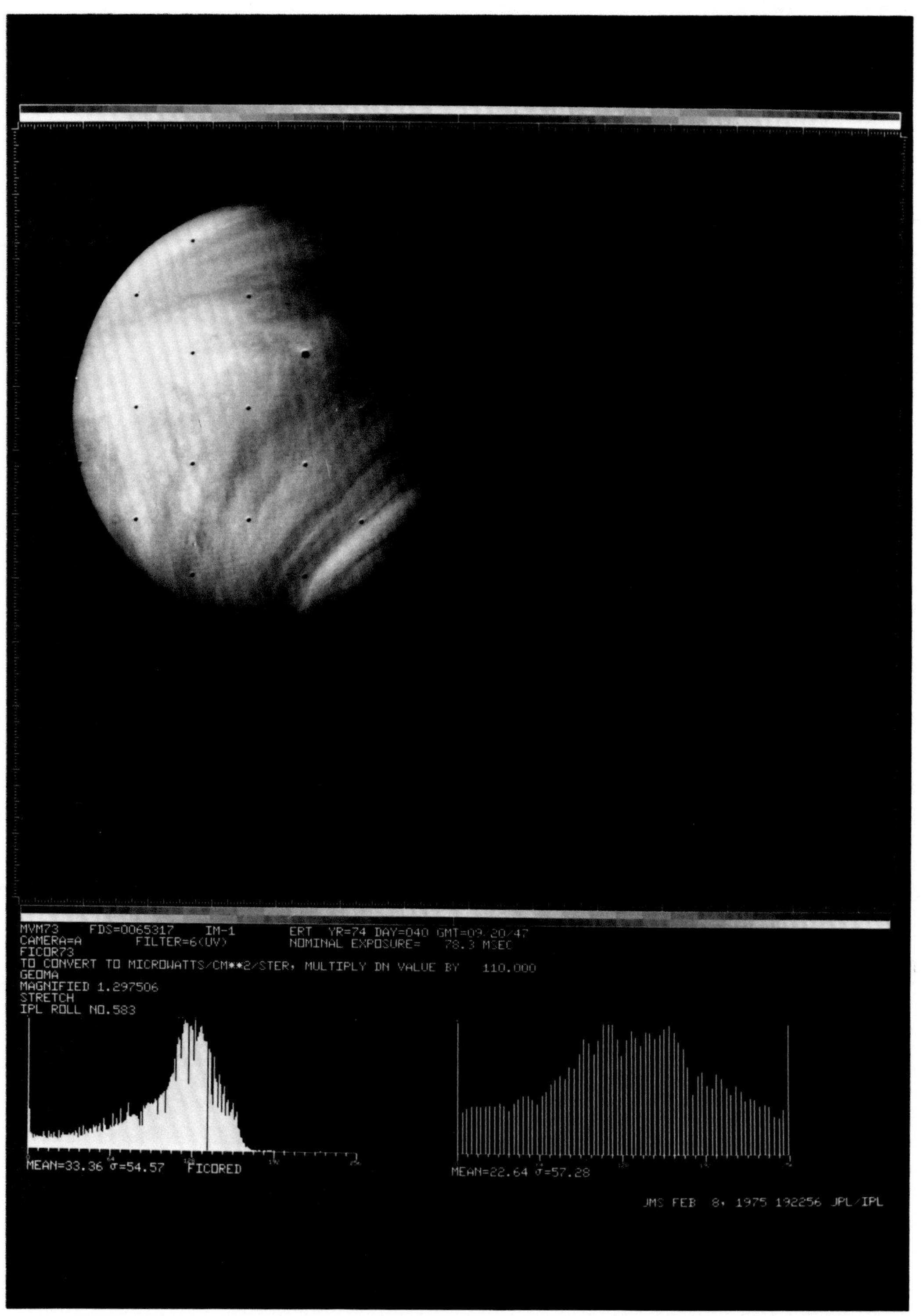
MVM73 FDS=0065317 IM-1 ERT YR=74 DAY=040 GMT=09/20/47
CAMERA=A FILTER=6(UV) NOMINAL EXPOSURE= 78.3 MSEC
FICOR73
TO CONVERT TO MICROWATTS/CM**2/STER, MULTIPLY DN VALUE BY 110.000
GEOMA
MAGNIFIED 1.297506
STRETCH
IPL ROLL NO.583
MEAN=33.36 σ=54.57 FICORED
MEAN=22.64 σ=57.28
JMS FEB 8, 1975 192256 JPL/IPL

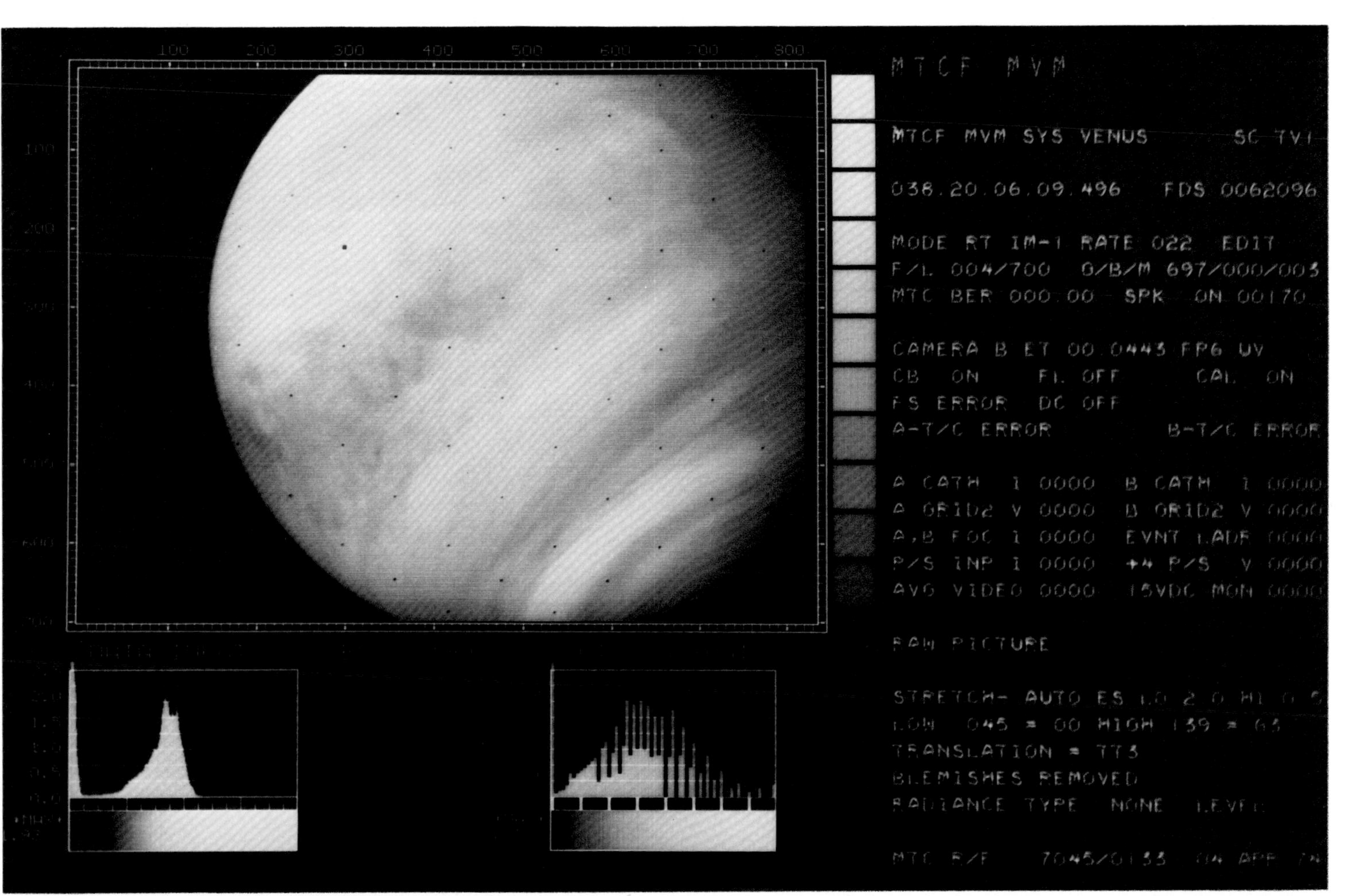

100 200 300 400 500 600 800
MTCF MVM
MTCF MVM SYS VENUS SC TV1
038.20.06.09.496 FDS 0062096
MODE RT IM-1 RATE 022 EDIT
F/L 004/700 G/B/M 697/000/003
MTC BER 000.00 SPK ON 00170
CAMERA B ET 00.0443 FP6 UV
CB ON FL OFF CAL ON
FS ERROR DC OFF
A-T/C ERROR B-T/C ERROR
A CATH I 0000 B CATH I 0000
A GRID2 V 0000 B GRID2 V 0000
A,B FOC I 0000 EVNT LADF 0000
P/S INP I 0000 +4 P/S V 0000
AVG VIDEO 0000 15VDC MON 0000
RAW PICTURE
STRETCH- AUTO ES
LOW 045 = 00 HIGH 139 = 63
TRANSLATION = TT3
BLEMISHES REMOVED
RADIANCE TYPE NONE LEVEL
MTC R/F 7045/0133

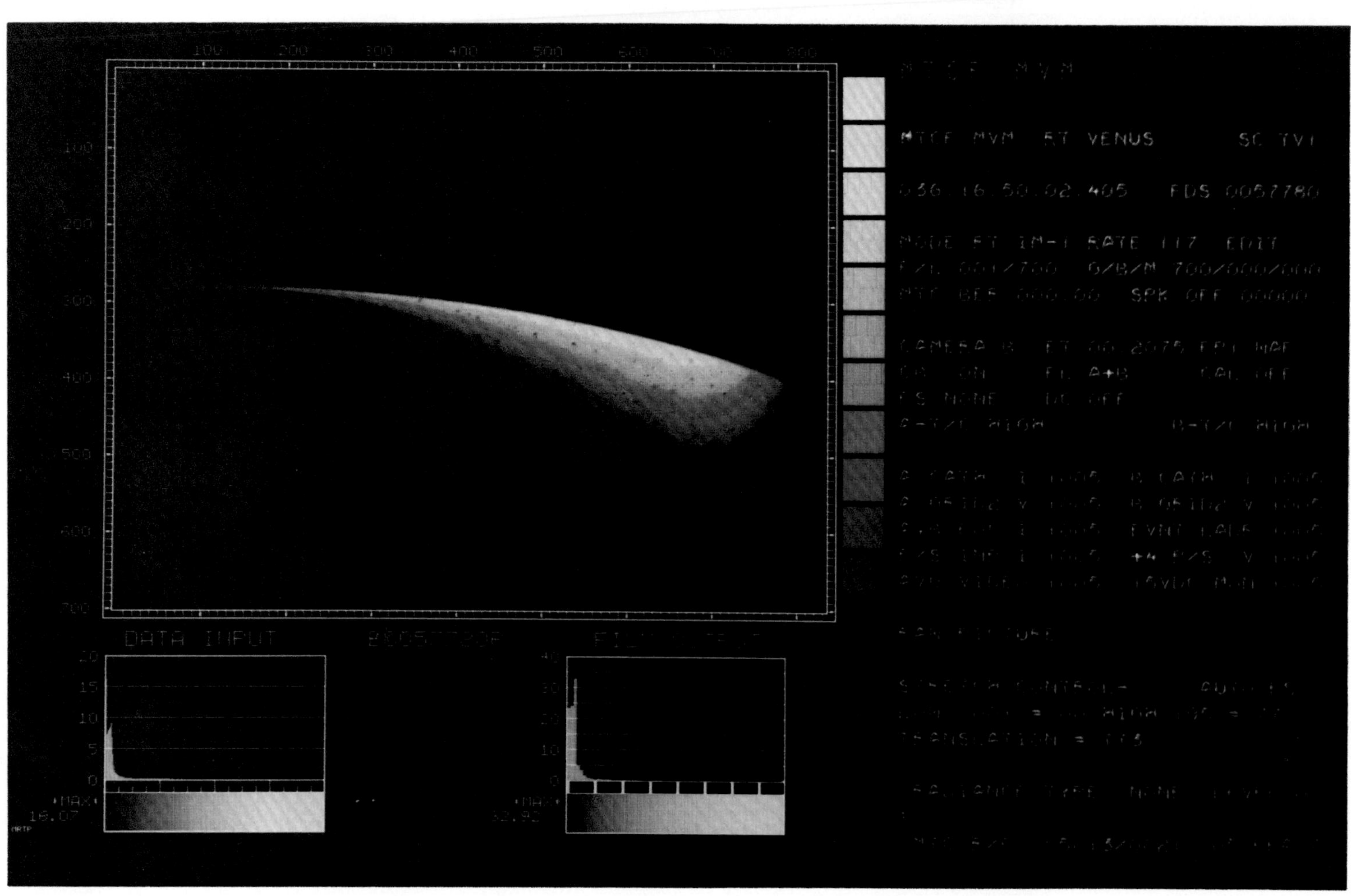
100 200 300 400 500 600 700 800
MTCF MVM
MTCF MVM 5T VENUS SC TV1
036 16 50 02.405 FDS 0057780
MODE FT IM-1 RATE 117 EDIT
F/L 001/700 G/B/M 700/000/000
MTF OFF 000.00 SPK OFF 00000
CAMERA B FT 00.2075 FP1 MAF
CA ON FL A+B CAL OFF
FS NONE DC OFF
A-T/C HIGH B-T/C HIGH
DATA INPUT

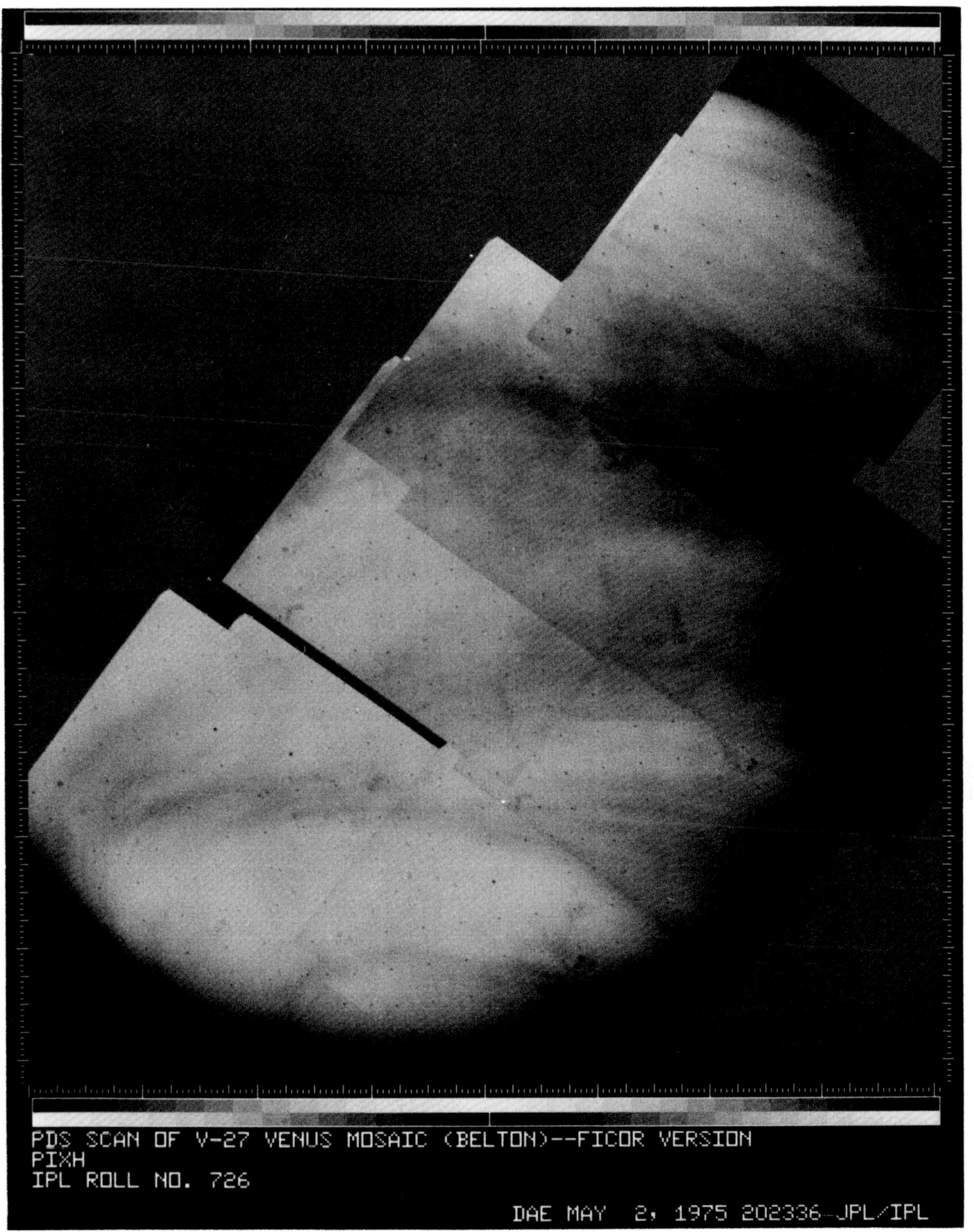
PDS SCAN OF V-27 VENUS MOSAIC (BELTON)--FICOR VERSION
PIXH
IPL ROLL NO. 726
DAE MAY 2, 1975 202336-JPL/IPL

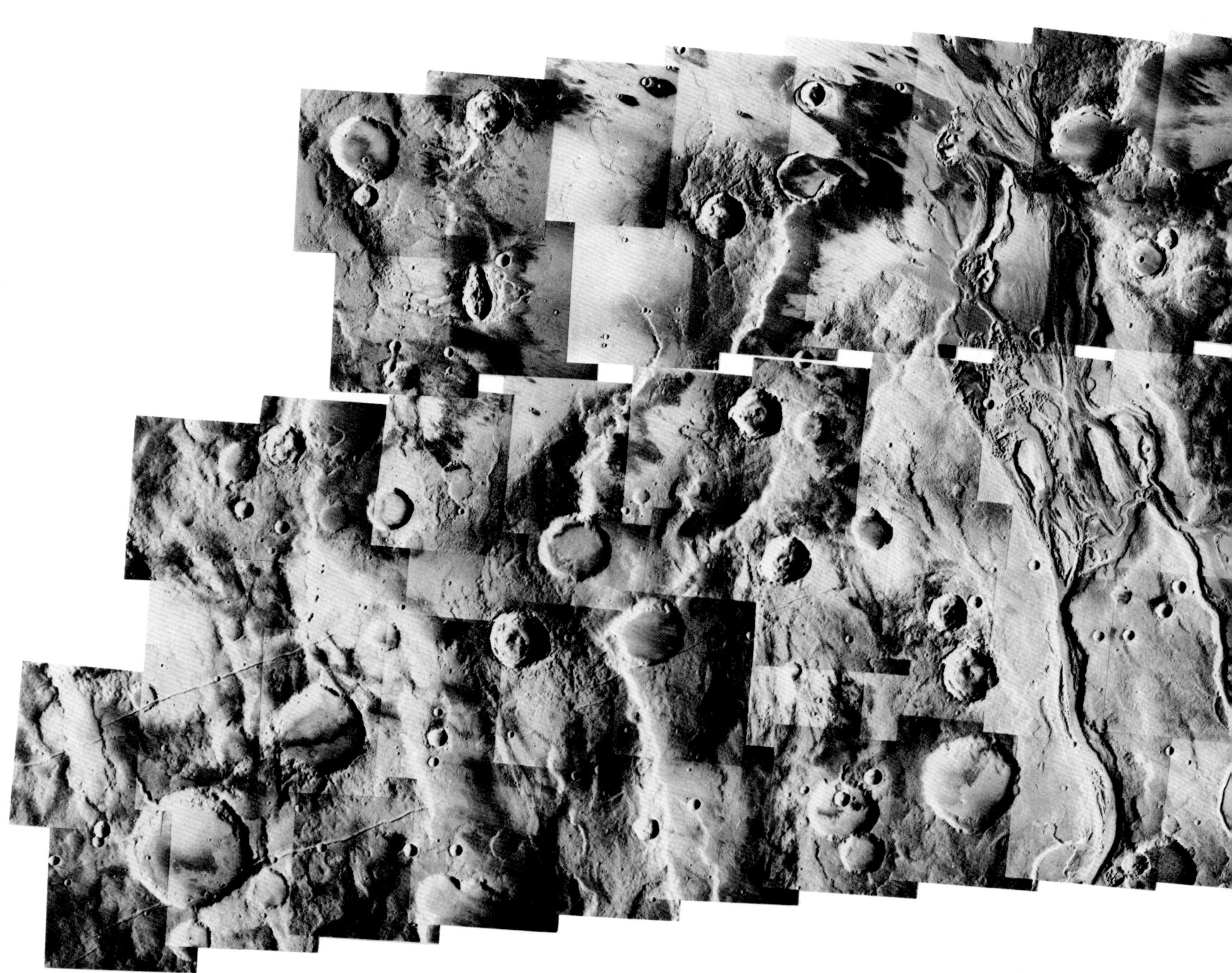

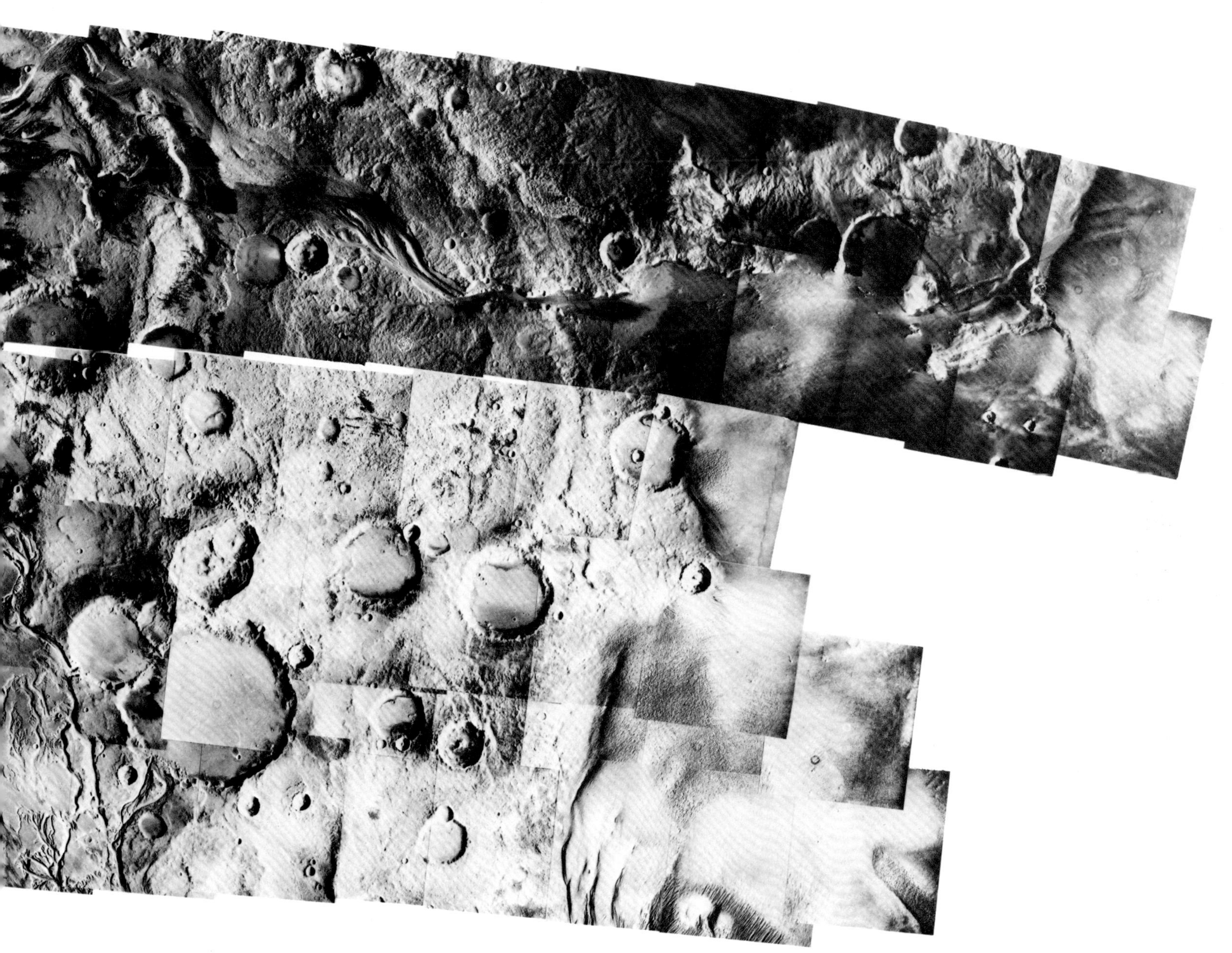

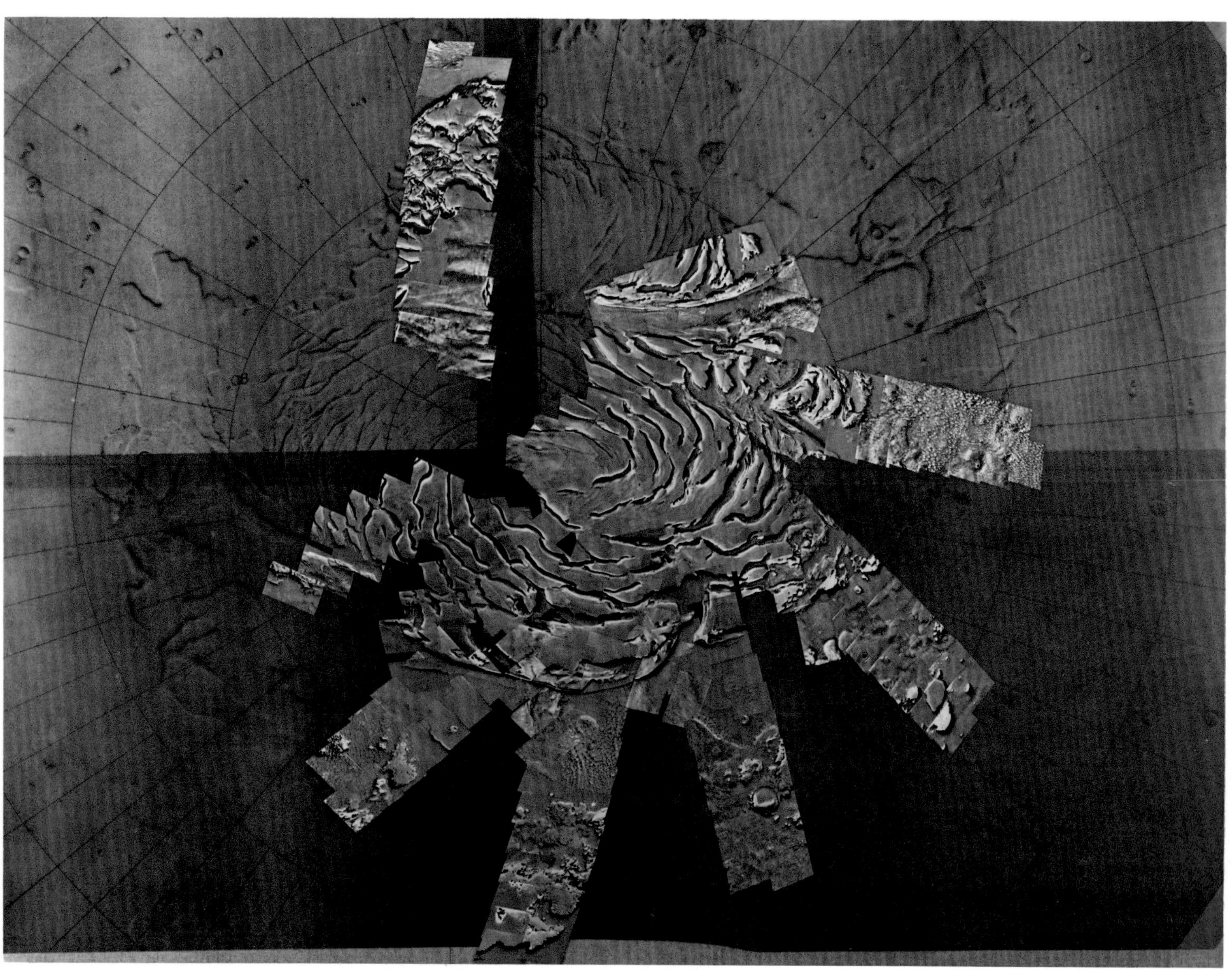

56 COMPOSITE VIEW, NORTHERN POLAR CAP, MARS

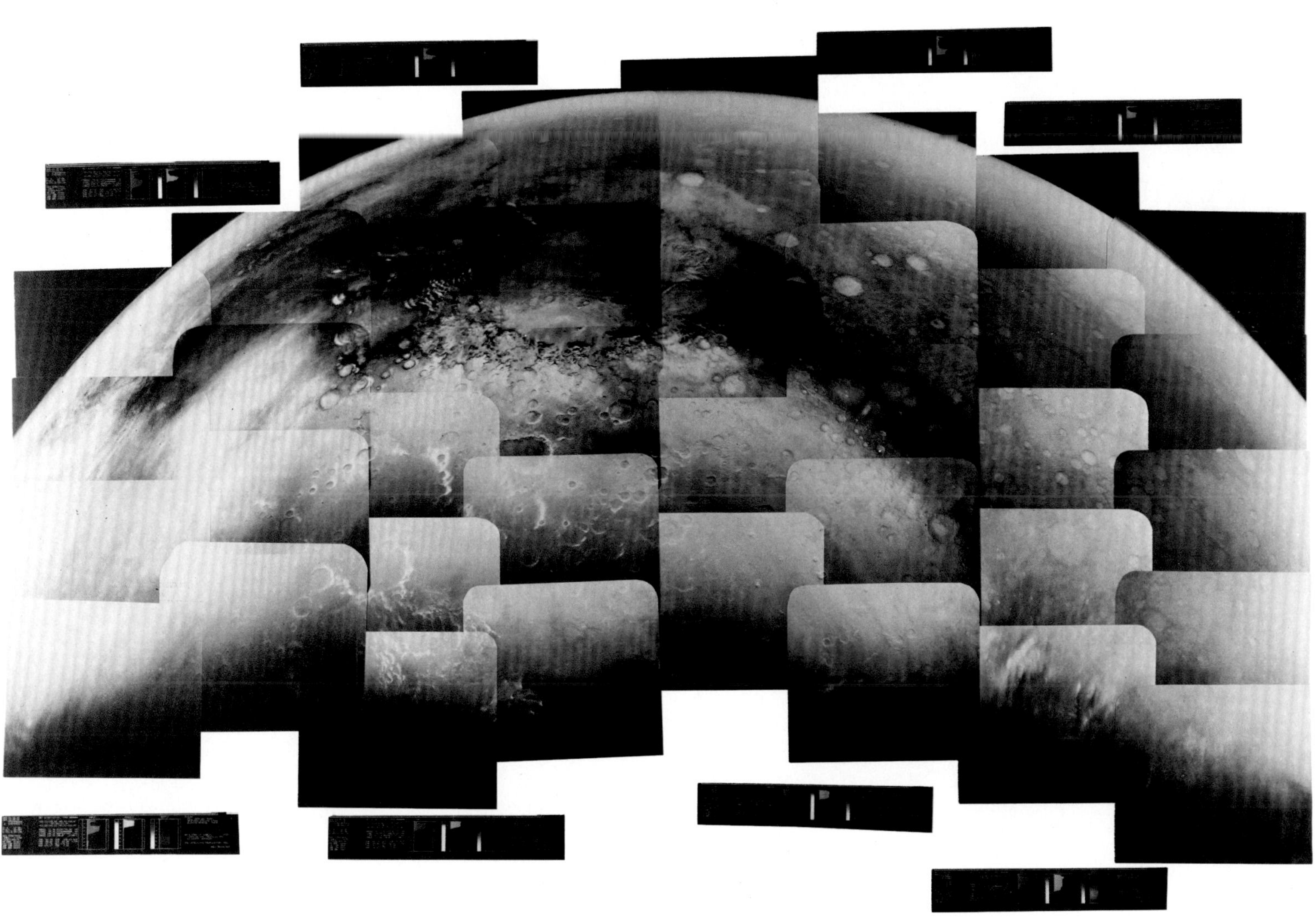

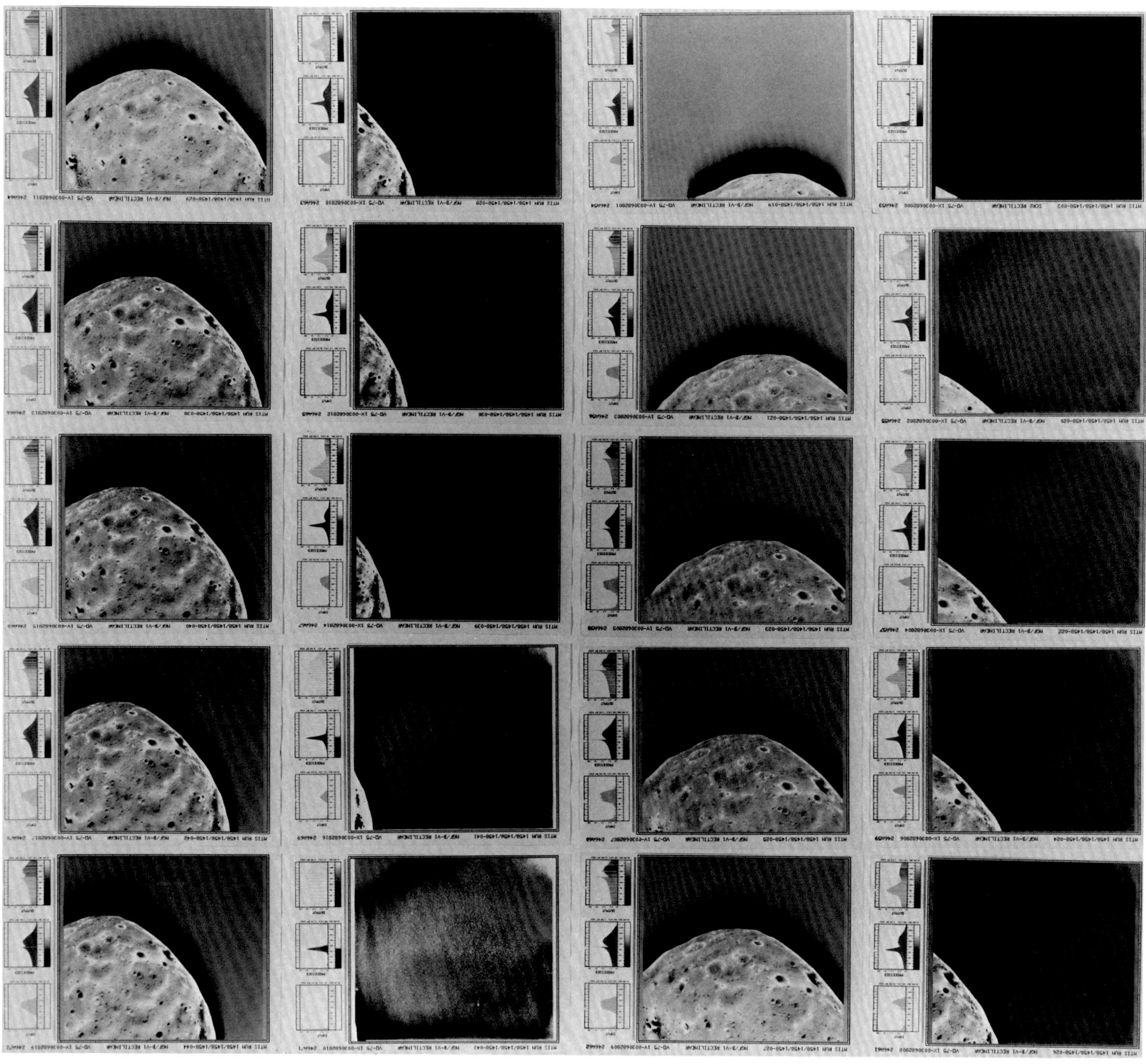

 SERIES, PHOBUS, A MOON OF MARS

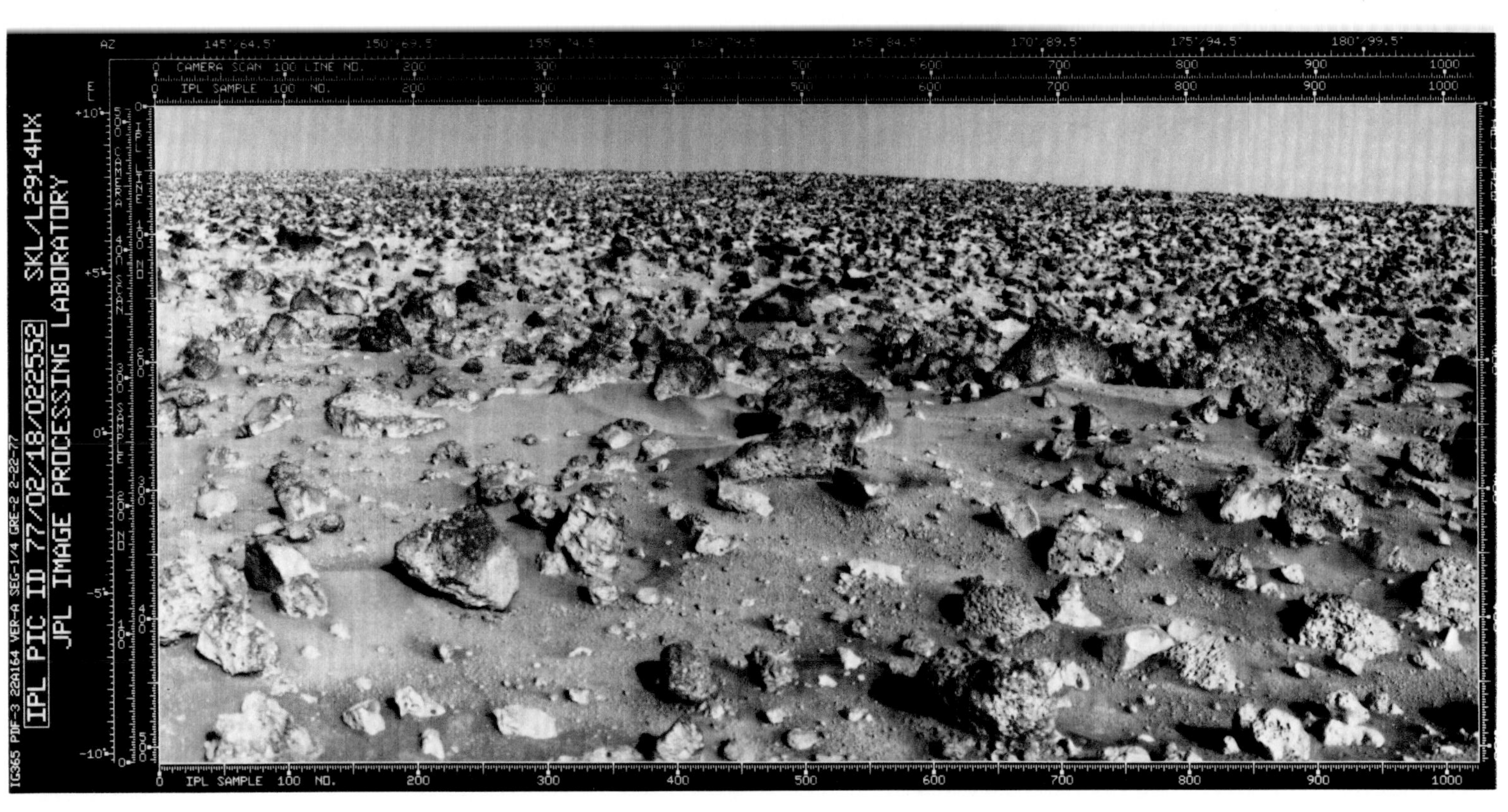
IPL PIC ID 77/02/18/022552
SKL/L2914HX
JPL IMAGE PROCESSING LABORATORY
CAMERA SCAN 100 LINE NO.
IPL SAMPLE 100 NO.

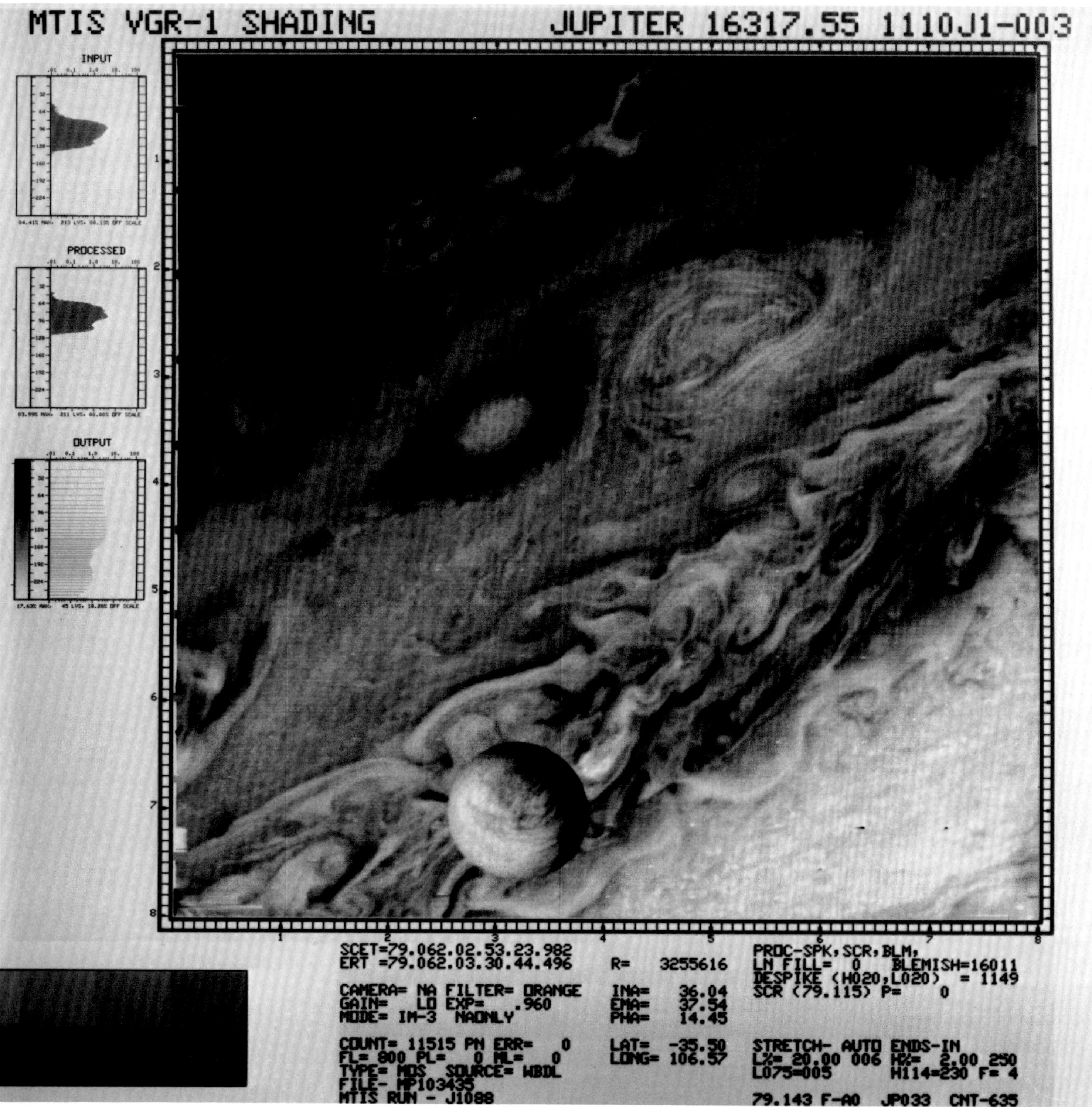
MTIS VGR-1 SHADING
JUPITER 16317.55 1110J1-003
INPUT
PROCESSED
OUTPUT
SCET=79.062.02.53.23.982
ERT =79.062.03.30.44.496
R= 3255616
PROC-SPK,SCR,BLM,
LN FILL= 0 BLEMISH=16011
DESPIKE (H020,L020) = 1149
SCR (79.115) P= 0
CAMERA= NA FILTER= ORANGE
GAIN= LO EXP= .960
MODE= IM-3 NAONLY
INA= 36.04
EMA= 37.54
PHA= 14.45
COUNT= 11515 PN ERR= 0
FL= 800 PL= 0 ML= 0
TYPE= MDS SOURCE= WBDL
FILE- MP103435
MTIS RUN - J1088
LAT= -35.50
LONG= 106.57
STRETCH- AUTO ENDS-IN
L%= 20.00 006 H%= 2.00 250
L075=005 H114=230 F= 4
79.143 F-A0 JP033 CNT-635

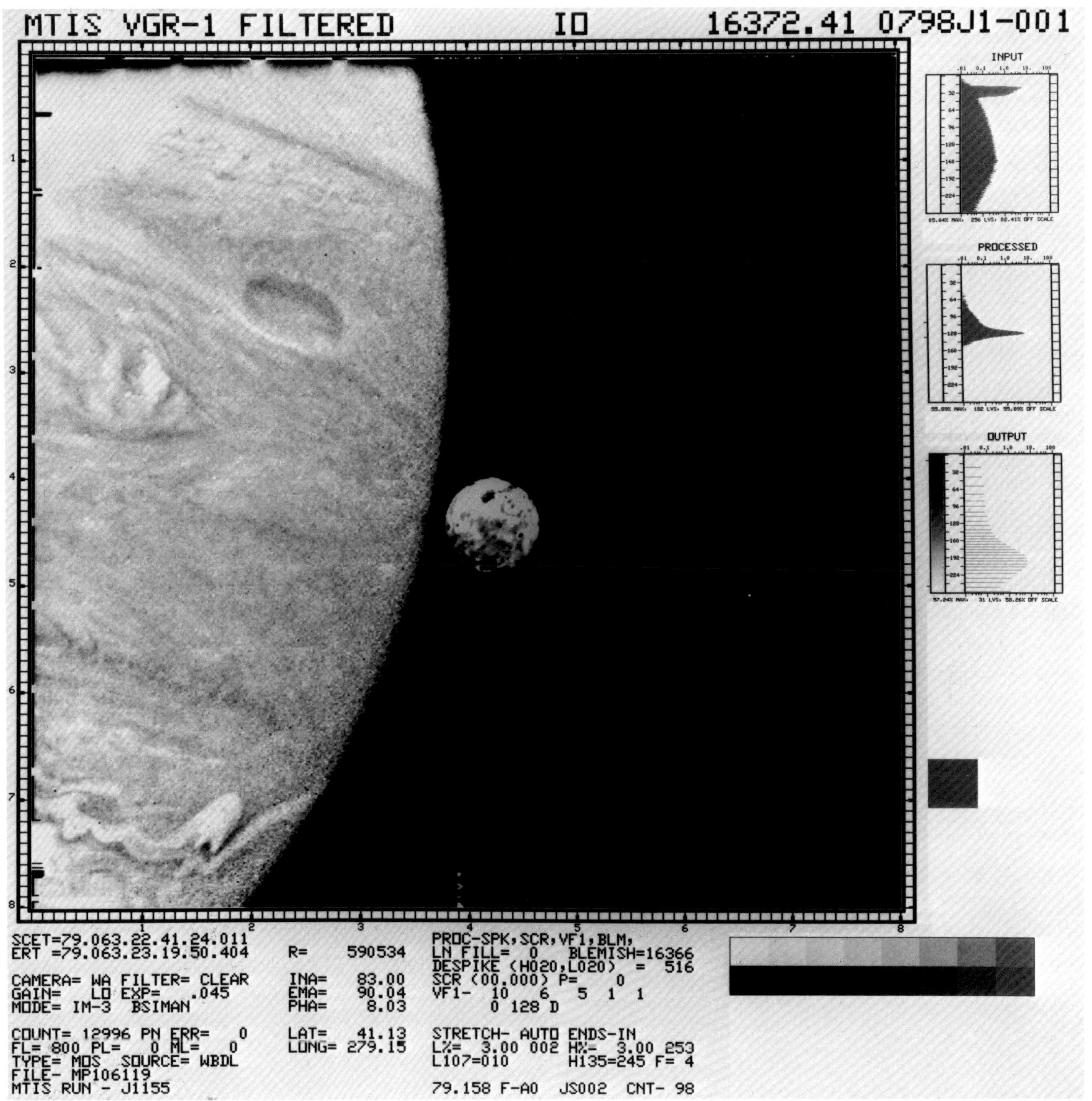
MTIS VGR-1 FILTERED IO 16372.41 0798J1-001
INPUT
PROCESSED
OUTPUT
SCET=79.063.22.41.24.011
ERT =79.063.23.19.50.404
R= 590534
CAMERA= WA FILTER= CLEAR
GAIN= LO EXP= .045
MODE= IM-3 BSIMAN
INA= 83.00
EMA= 90.04
PHA= 8.03
COUNT= 12996 PN ERR= 0
FL= 800 PL= 0 ML= 0
TYPE= MOS SOURCE= WBDL
FILE- MP106119
MTIS RUN - J1155
LAT= 41.13
LONG= 279.15
PROC-SPK,SCR,VF1,BLM,
LN FILL= 0 BLEMISH=16366
DESPIKE (H020,L020) = 516
SCR (00,000) P= 0
VF1- 10 6 5 1 1
0 128 D
STRETCH- AUTO ENDS-IN
L%= 3.00 002 H%= 3.00 253
L107=010 H135=245 F= 4
79.158 F-A0 JS002 CNT- 98

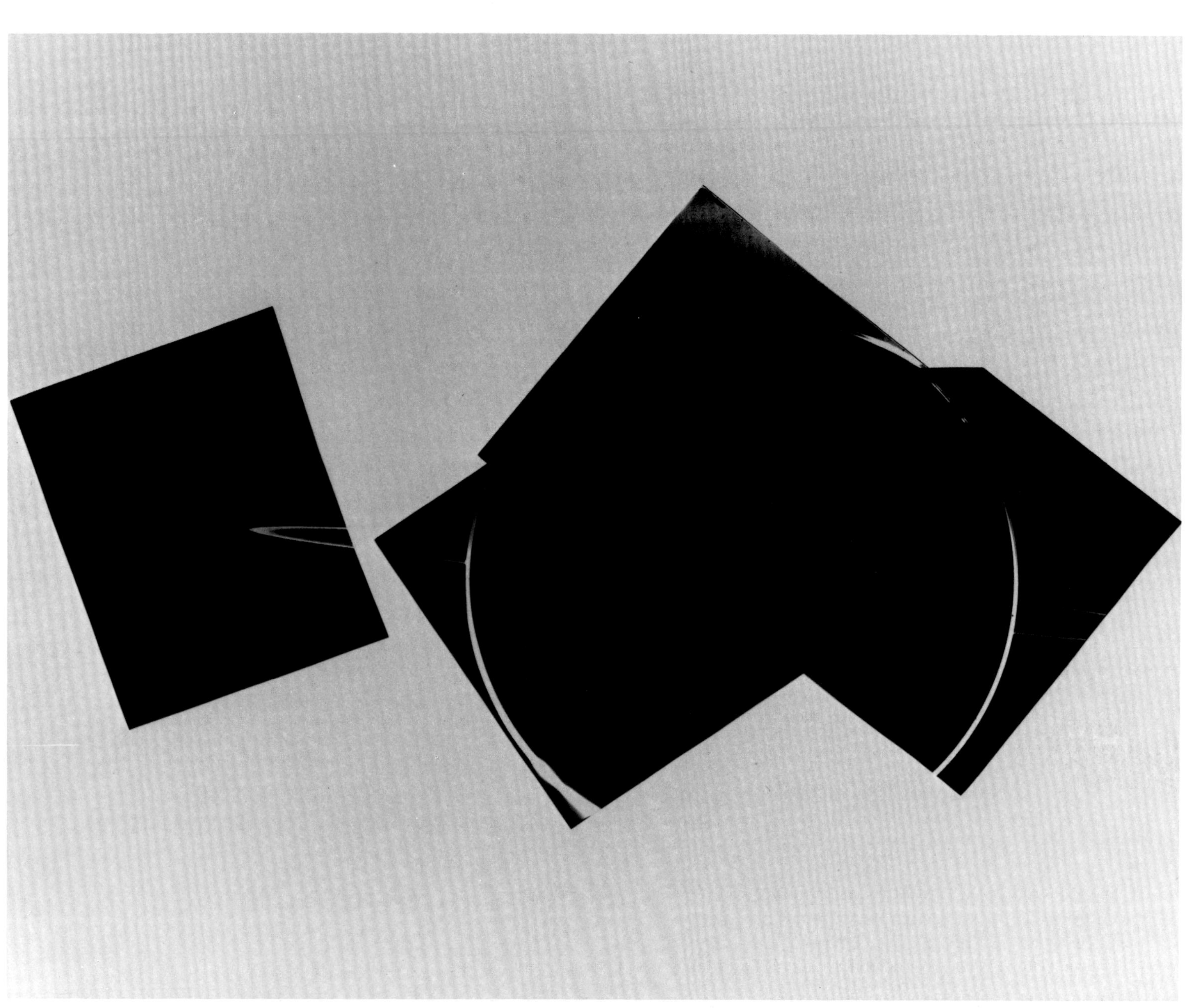

62 RING OF PARTICLES ORBITING JUPITER

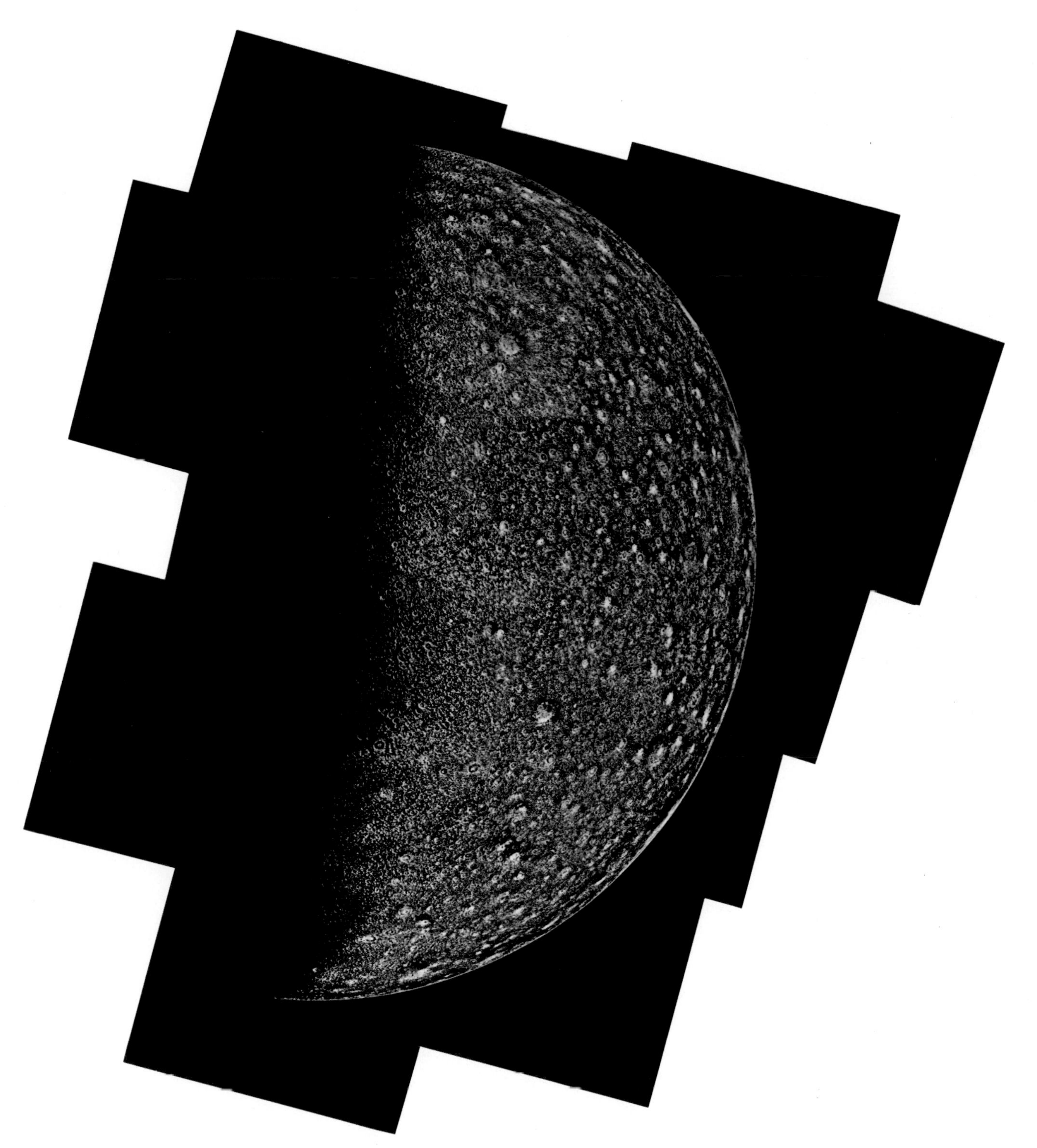

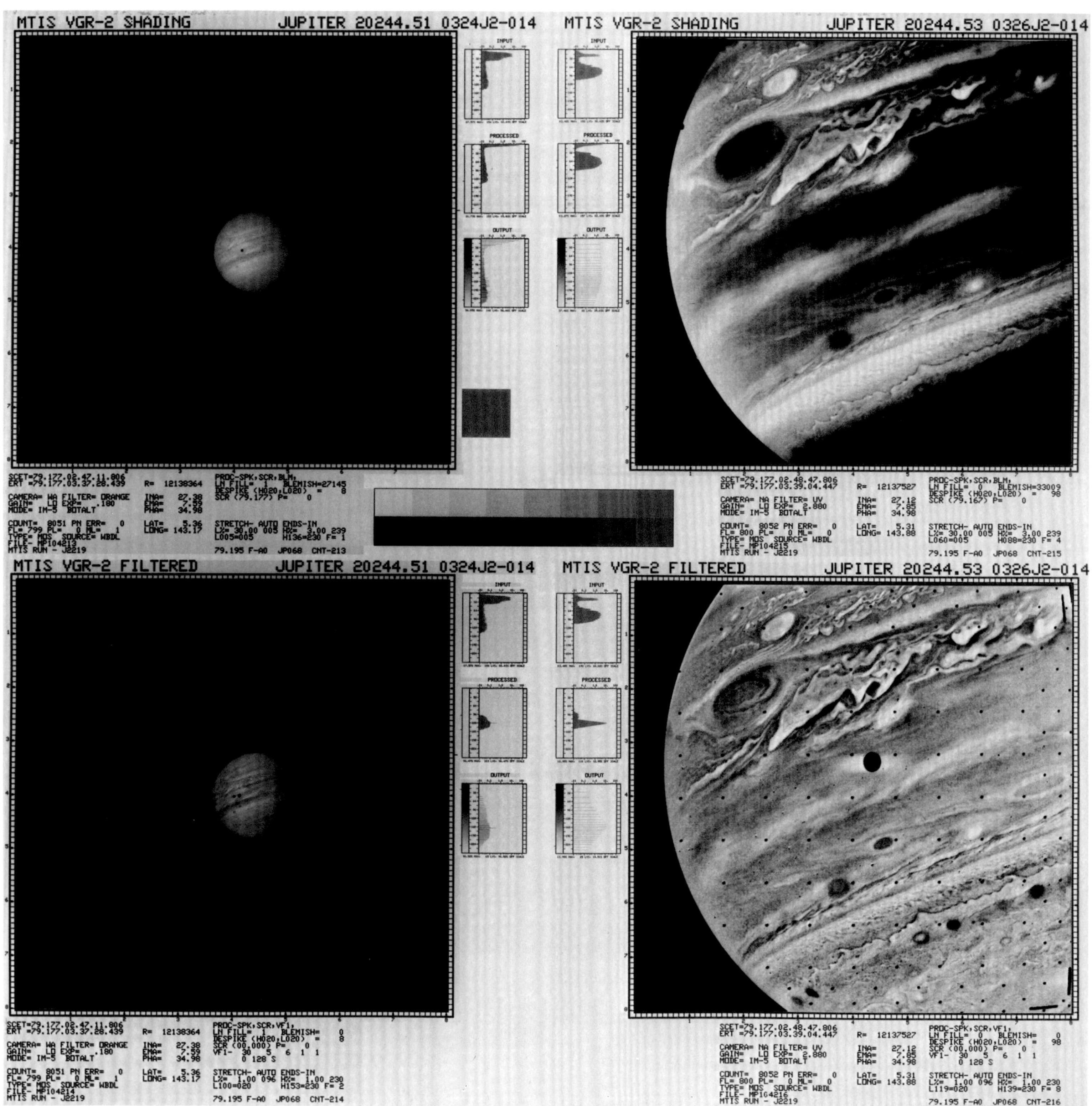

MTIS VGR-2 SHADING
JUPITER 20244.51 0324J2-014
MTIS VGR-2 SHADING
JUPITER 20244.53 0326J2-014
INPUT
PROCESSED
OUTPUT
SCET=79.177.02.47.11.806
ERT =79.177.03.37.28.439
R= 12138364
PROC-SPK,SCR,BLM,
LN FILL= 1 BLEMISH=27145
DESPIKE (H020,L020) = 8
SCR (79.177) P= 0
CAMERA= WA FILTER= ORANGE
GAIN= LO EXP= .180
MODE= IM-5 BOTALT
INA= 27.38
EMA= 7.59
PHA= 34.98
COUNT= 8051 PN ERR= 0
FL= 799 PL= 0 ML= 1
TYPE= MOS SOURCE= WBDL
FILE- MP104213
MTIS RUN - J2219
LAT= 5.36
LONG= 143.17
STRETCH- AUTO ENDS-IN
L%= 30.00 005 H%= 3.00 239
L005=005 H136=230 F= 1
79.195 F-A0 JP068 CNT-213
SCET=79.177.02.48.47.806
ERT =79.177.03.39.04.447
R= 12137527
PROC-SPK,SCR,BLM,
LN FILL= 0 BLEMISH=33009
DESPIKE (H020,L020) = 98
SCR (79.167) P= 0
CAMERA= NA FILTER= UV
GAIN= LO EXP= 2.880
MODE= IM-5 BOTALT
INA= 27.12
EMA= 7.85
PHA= 34.98
COUNT= 8052 PN ERR= 0
FL= 800 PL= 0 ML= 0
TYPE= MOS SOURCE= WBDL
FILE- MP104215
MTIS RUN - J2219
LAT= 5.31
LONG= 143.88
STRETCH- AUTO ENDS-IN
L%= 30.00 005 H%= 3.00 239
L060=005 H088=230 F= 4
79.195 F-A0 JP068 CNT-215
MTIS VGR-2 FILTERED
JUPITER 20244.51 0324J2-014
MTIS VGR-2 FILTERED
JUPITER 20244.53 0326J2-014
INPUT
PROCESSED
OUTPUT
SCET=79.177.02.47.11.806
ERT =79.177.03.37.28.439
R= 12138364
PROC-SPK,SCR,VF1,
LN FILL= 1 BLEMISH= 0
DESPIKE (H020,L020) = 8
SCR (00,000) P= 0
VF1- 30 5 6 1 1
0 128 S
CAMERA= WA FILTER= ORANGE
GAIN= LO EXP= .180
MODE= IM-5 BOTALT
INA= 27.38
EMA= 7.59
PHA= 34.98
COUNT= 8051 PN ERR= 0
FL= 799 PL= 0 ML= 1
TYPE= MOS SOURCE= WBDL
FILE- MP104214
MTIS RUN - J2219
LAT= 5.36
LONG= 143.17
STRETCH- AUTO ENDS-IN
L%= 1.00 096 H%= 1.00 230
L100=020 H153=230 F= 2
79.195 F-A0 JP068 CNT-214
SCET=79.177.02.48.47.806
ERT =79.177.03.39.04.447
R= 12137527
PROC-SPK,SCR,VF1,
LN FILL= 0 BLEMISH= 0
DESPIKE (H020,L020) = 98
SCR (00,000) P= 0
VF1- 30 5 6 1 1
0 128 S
CAMERA= NA FILTER= UV
GAIN= LO EXP= 2.880
MODE= IM-5 BOTALT
INA= 27.12
EMA= 7.85
PHA= 34.98
COUNT= 8052 PN ERR= 0
FL= 800 PL= 0 ML= 0
TYPE= MOS SOURCE= WBDL
FILE- MP104216
MTIS RUN - J2219
LAT= 5.31
LONG= 143.88
STRETCH- AUTO ENDS-IN
L%= 1.00 096 H%= 1.00 230
L119=020 H139=230 F= 8
79.195 F-A0 JP068 CNT-216

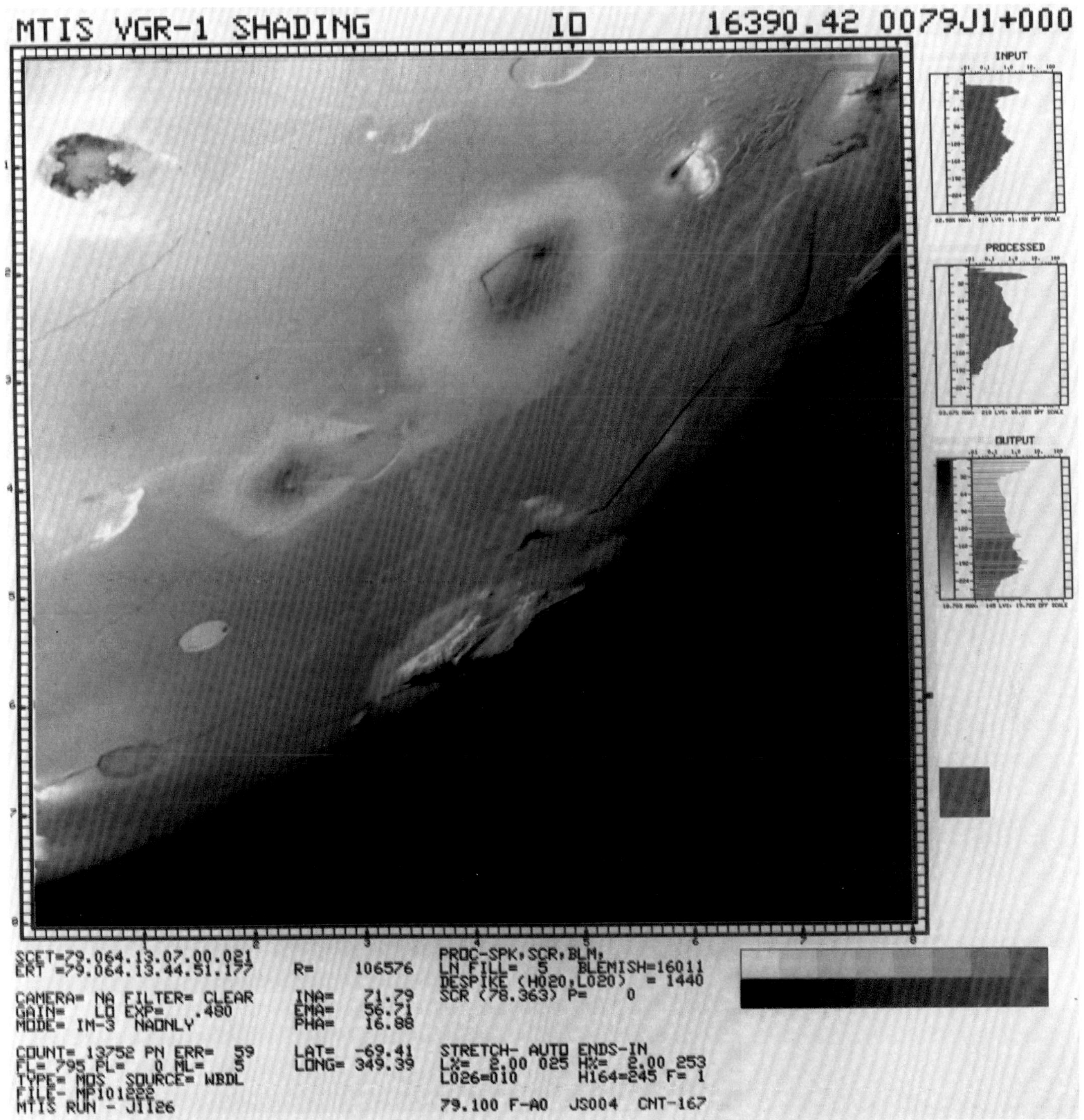
MTIS VGR-1 SHADING IO 16390.42 0079J1+000
INPUT
PROCESSED
OUTPUT
SCET=79.064.13.07.00.021
ERT =79.064.13.44.51.177
R= 106576
PROC-SPK,SCR,BLM,
LN FILL= 5 BLEMISH=16011
DESPIKE (H020,L020) = 1440
SCR (78.363) P= 0
CAMERA= NA FILTER= CLEAR
GAIN= LO EXP= .480
MODE= IM-3 NAONLY
INA= 71.79
EMA= 56.71
PHA= 16.88
COUNT= 13752 PN ERR= 59
FL= 795 PL= 0 ML= 5
TYPE= MDS SOURCE= WBDL
FILE= MP101222
MTIS RUN - JI126
LAT= -69.41
LONG= 349.39
STRETCH- AUTO ENDS-IN
LX= 2.00 025 HX= 2.00 253
L026=010 H164=245 F= 1
79.100 F-A0 JS004 CNT-167

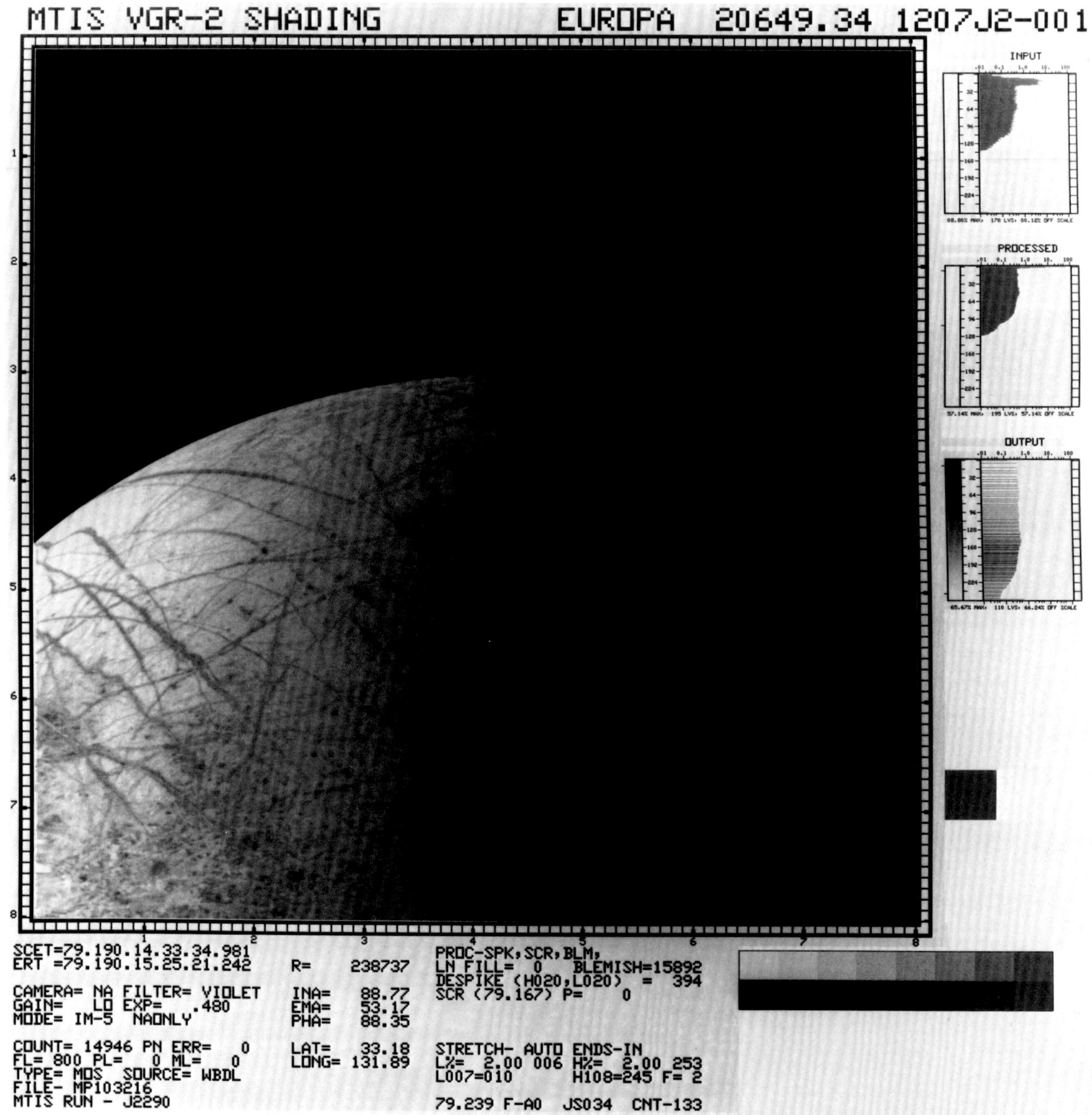
MTIS VGR-2 SHADING EUROPA 20649.34 1207J2-001
INPUT
PROCESSED
OUTPUT
SCET=79.190.14.33.34.981
ERT =79.190.15.25.21.242
R= 238737
CAMERA= NA FILTER= VIOLET
GAIN= LO EXP= .480
MODE= IM-5 NAONLY
INA= 88.77
EMA= 53.17
PHA= 88.35
COUNT= 14946 PN ERR= 0
FL= 800 PL= 0 ML= 0
TYPE= MDS SOURCE= WBDL
FILE- MP103216
MTIS RUN - J2290
LAT= 33.18
LONG= 131.89
PROC-SPK,SCR,BLM,
LN FILL= 0 BLEMISH=15892
DESPIKE (H020,L020) = 394
SCR (79.167) P= 0
STRETCH- AUTO ENDS-IN
L%= 2.00 006 H%= 2.00 253
L007=010 H108=245 F= 2
79.239 F-A0 JS034 CNT-133

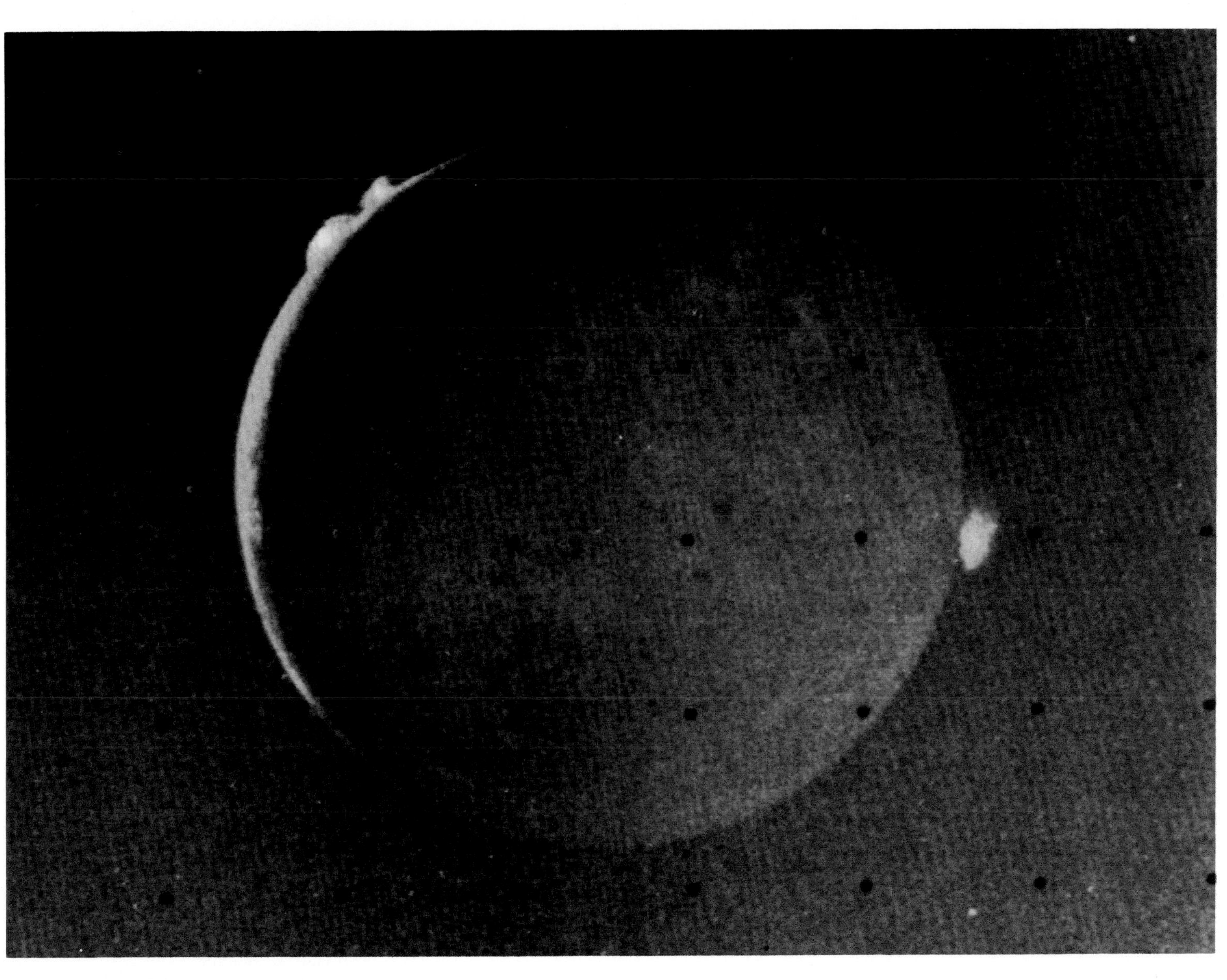

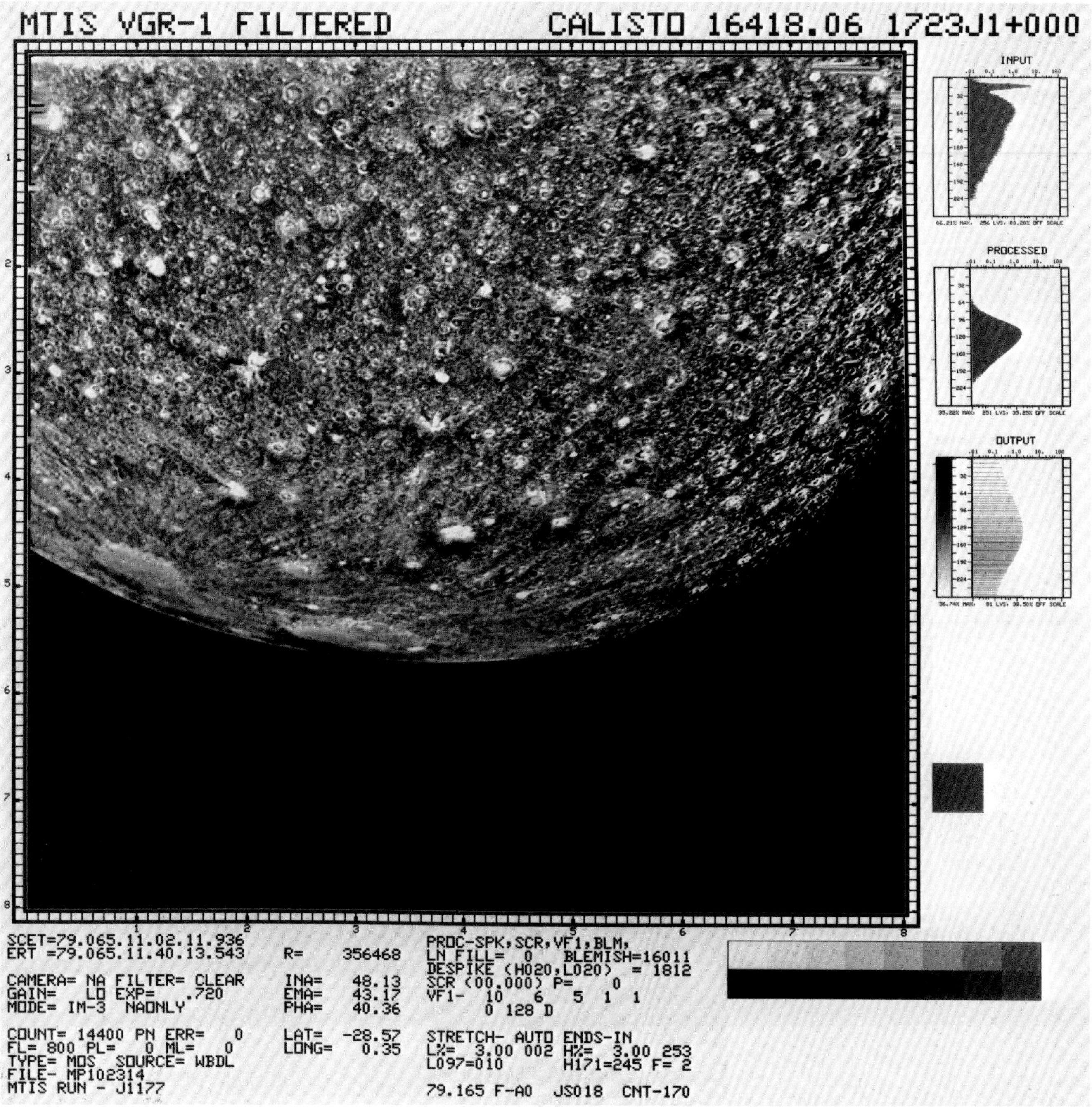
MTIS VGR-1 FILTERED
CALISTO 16418.06 1723J1+000
INPUT
PROCESSED
OUTPUT
SCET=79.065.11.02.11.936
ERT =79.065.11.40.13.543
CAMERA= NA FILTER= CLEAR
GAIN= LO EXP= .720
MODE= IM-3 NAONLY
COUNT= 14400 PN ERR= 0
FL= 800 PL= 0 ML= 0
TYPE= MOS SOURCE= WBDL
FILE- MP102314
MTIS RUN - J1177
R= 356468
INA= 48.13
EMA= 43.17
PHA= 40.36
LAT= -28.57
LONG= 0.35
PROC-SPK,SCR,VF1,BLM,
LN FILL= 0 BLEMISH=16011
DESPIKE (H020,L020) = 1812
SCR (00,000) P= 0
VF1- 10 6 5 1 1
0 128 D
STRETCH- AUTO ENDS-IN
L%= 3.00 002 H%= 3.00 253
L097=010 H171=245 F= 2
79.165 F-A0 JS018 CNT-170

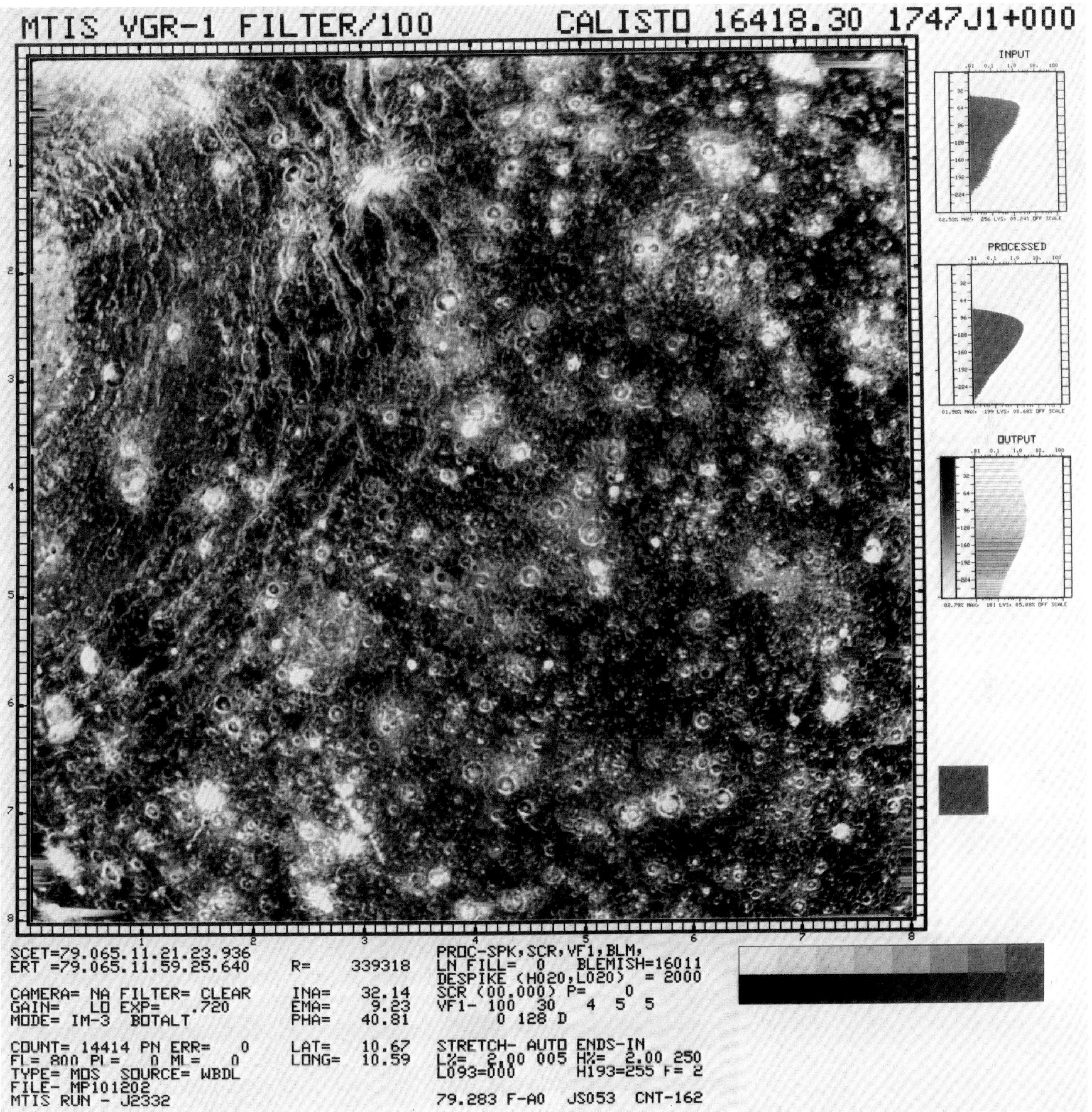

600 MILE VIEW ACROSS CALLISTO, A MOON OF JUPITER

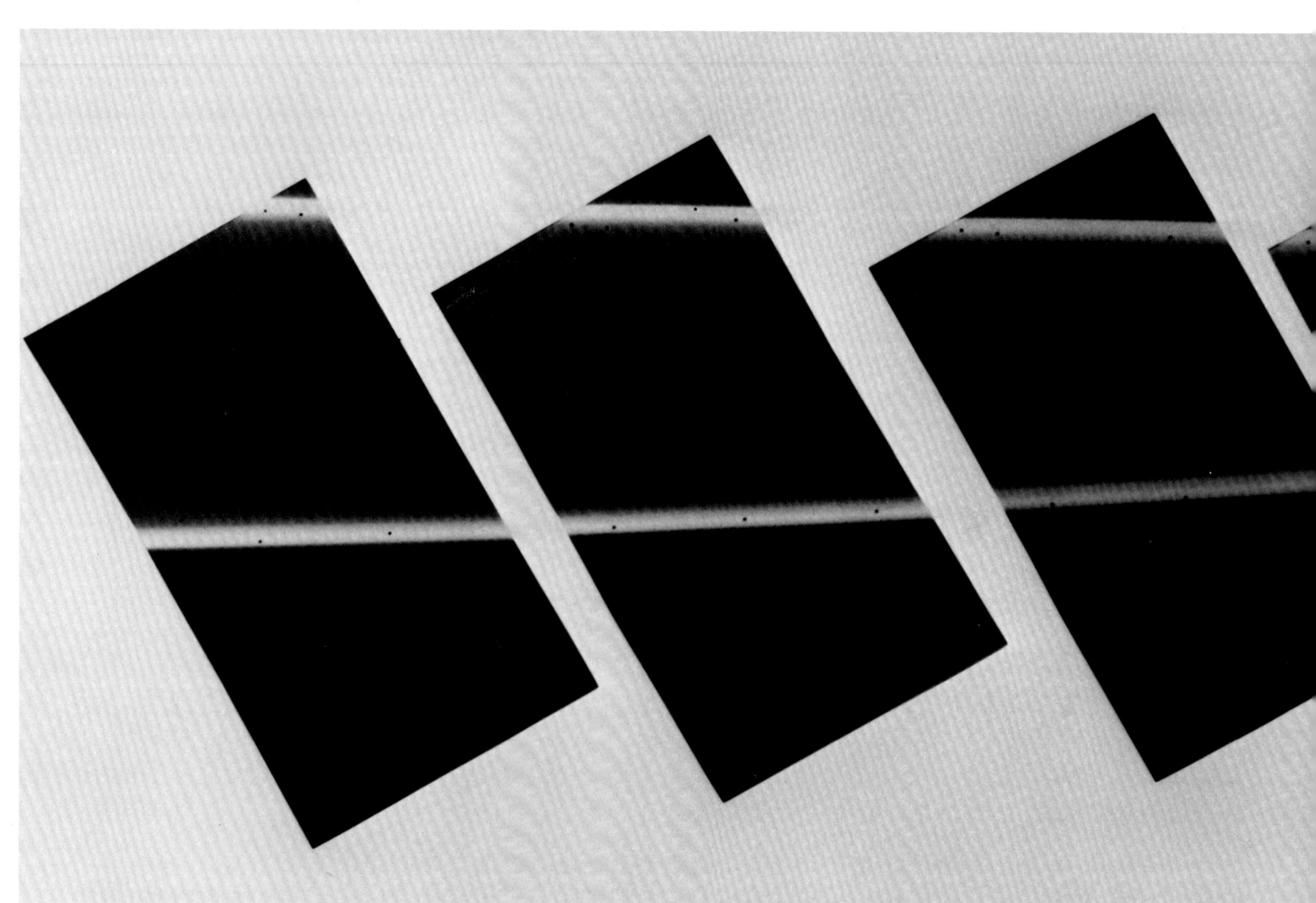

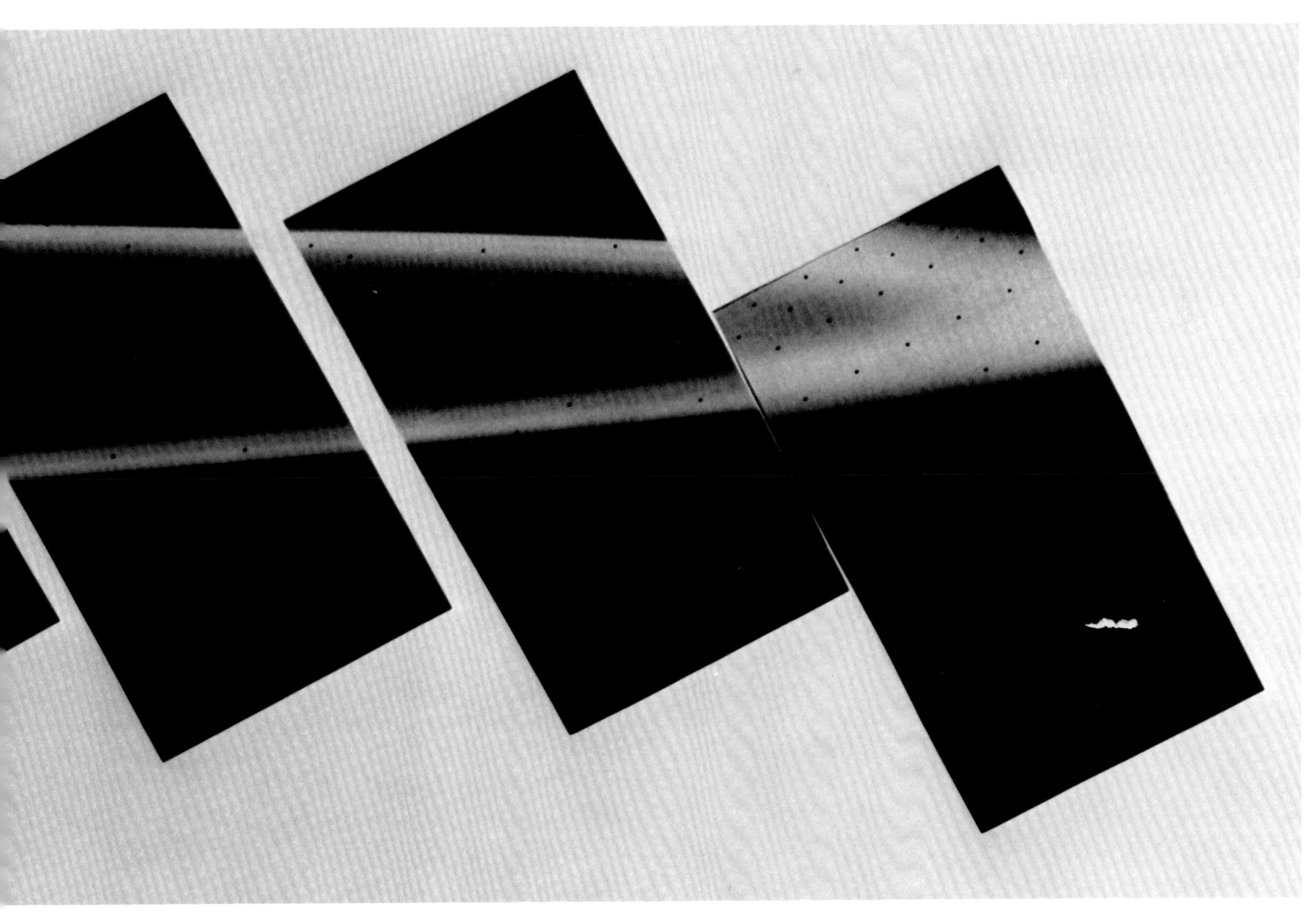

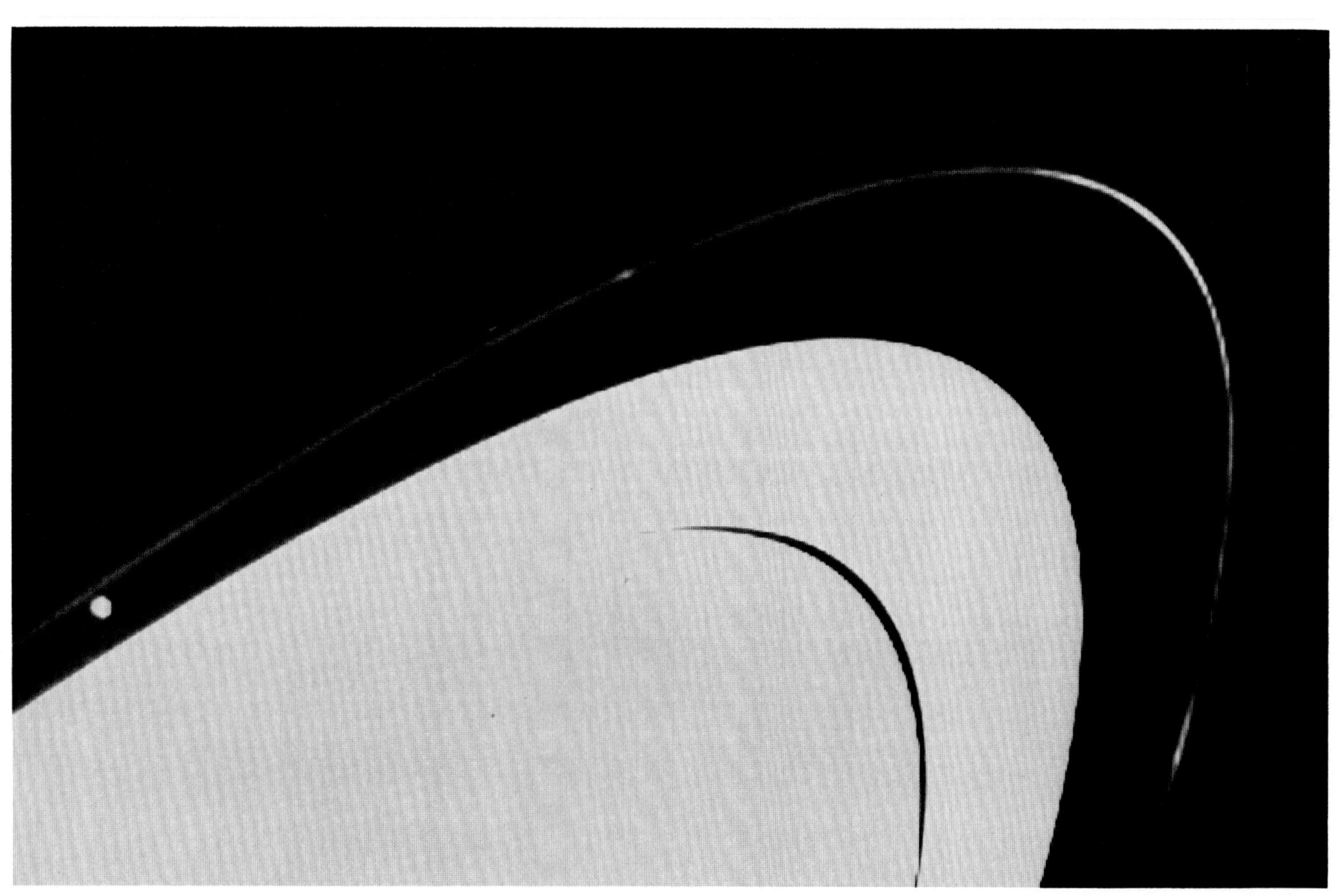

72 SATELLITE DISCOVERED IN THE GAP BETWEEN TWO OF SATURN'S RINGS

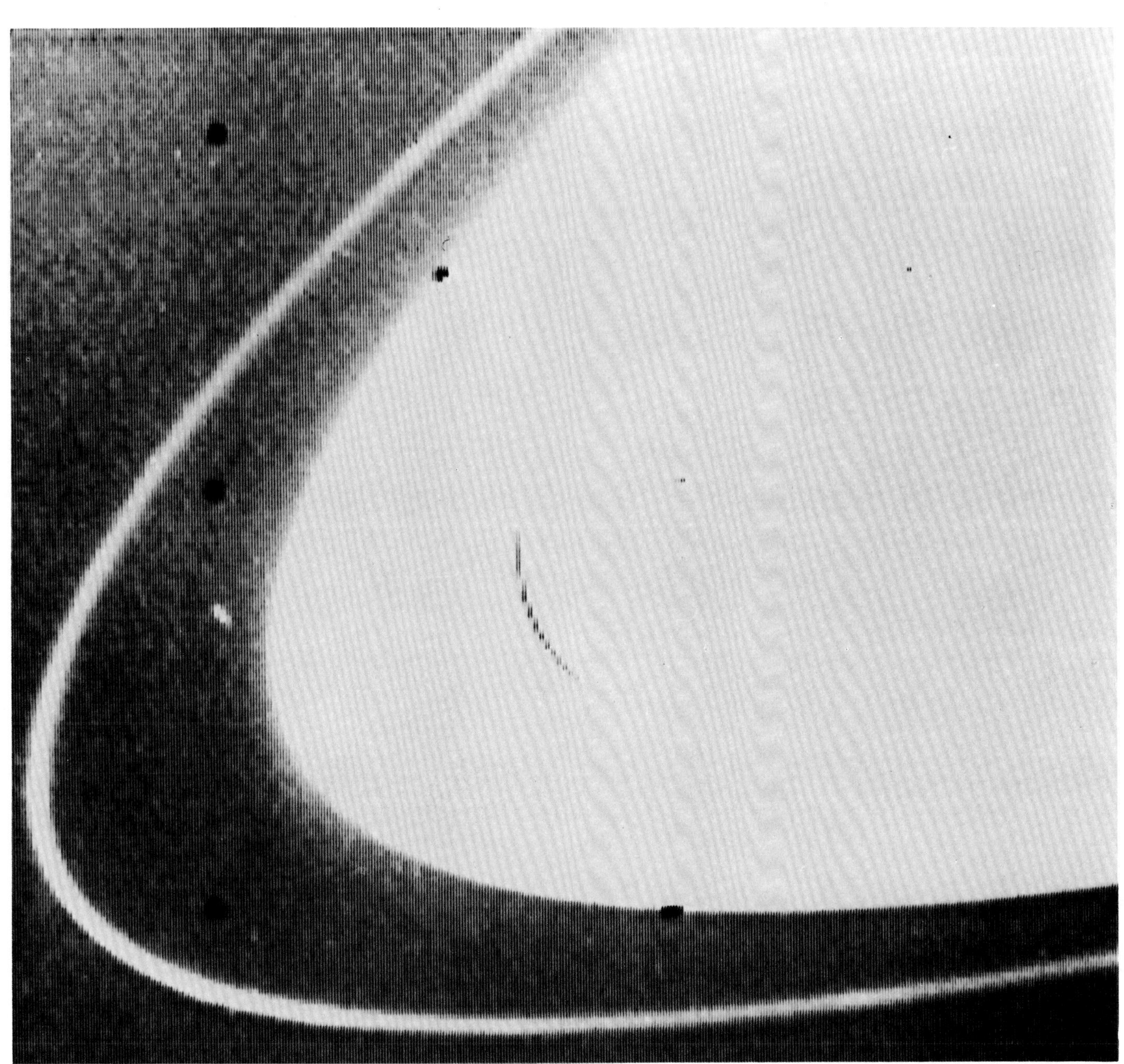

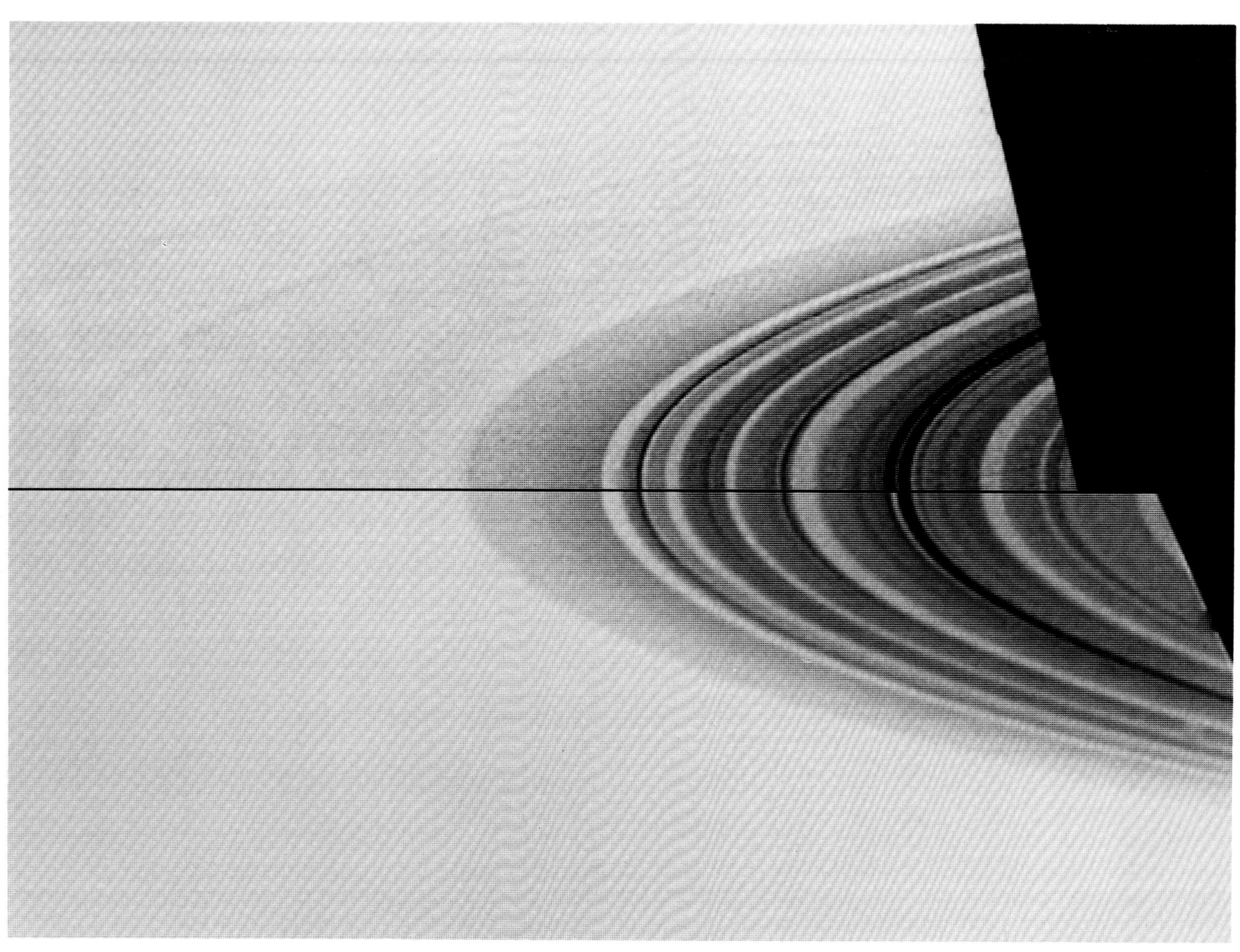

74 COMPOSITE OF A RING OF SATURN

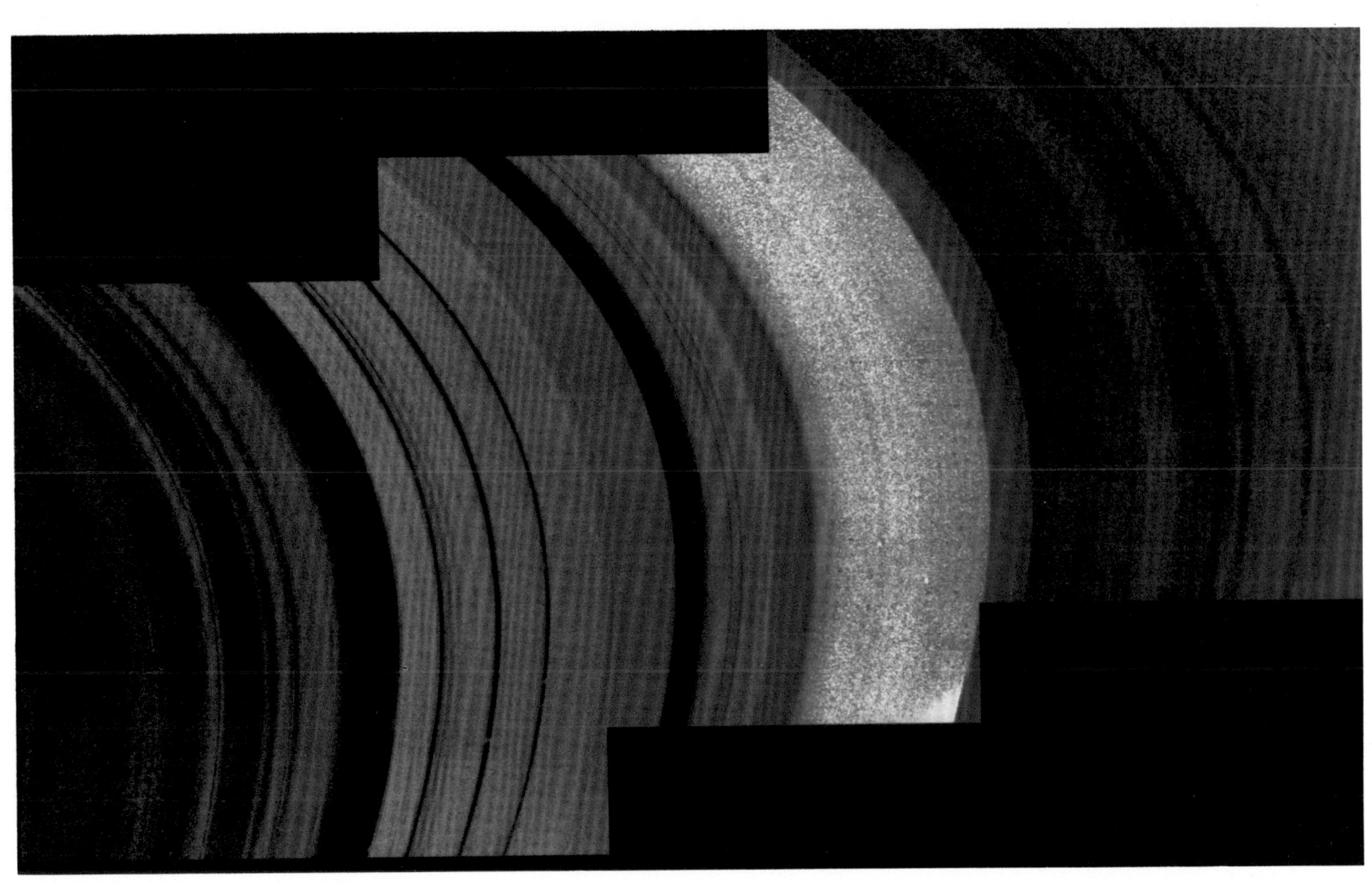

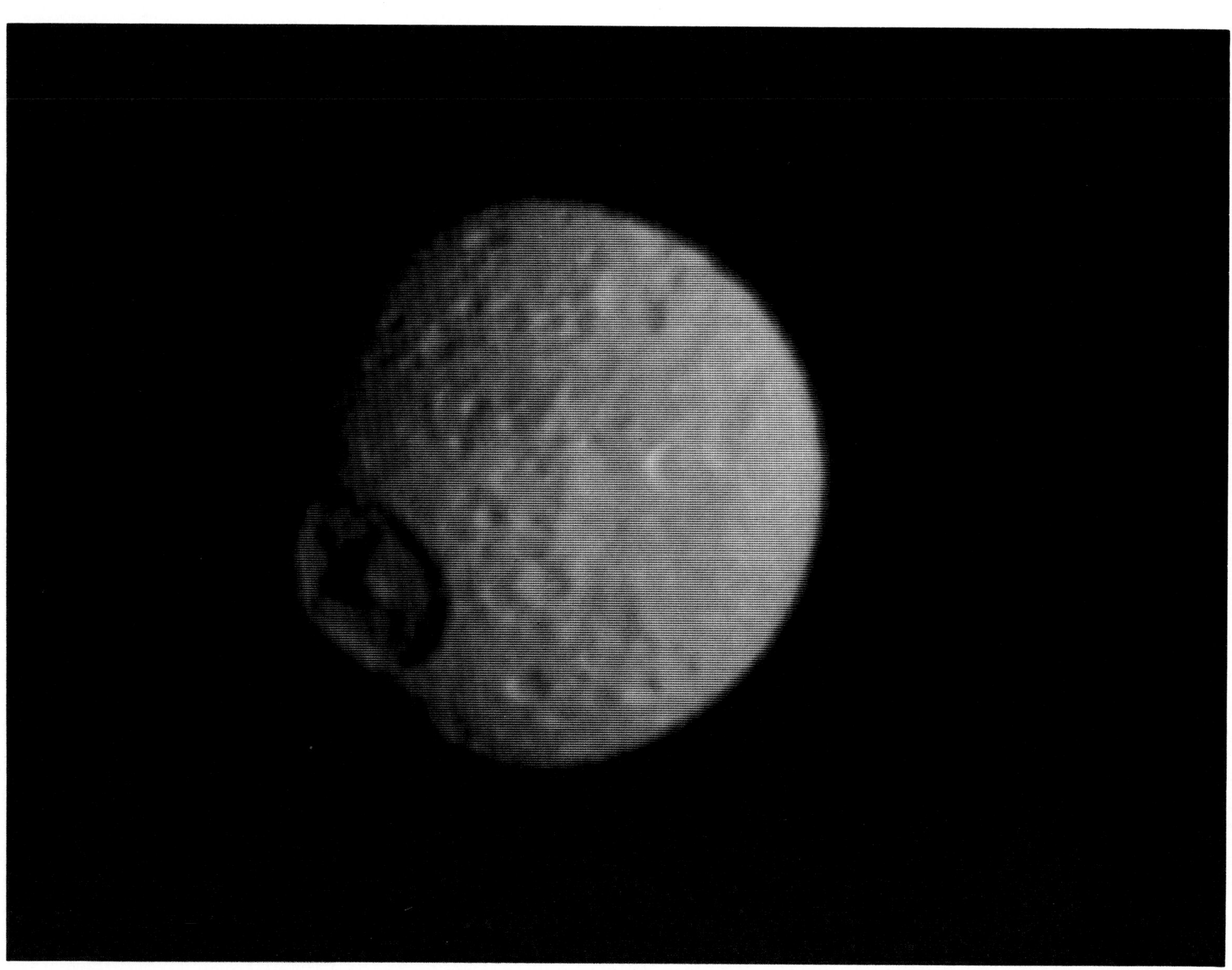

 60 MILE CRATER ON MIMAS, A MOON OF SATURN

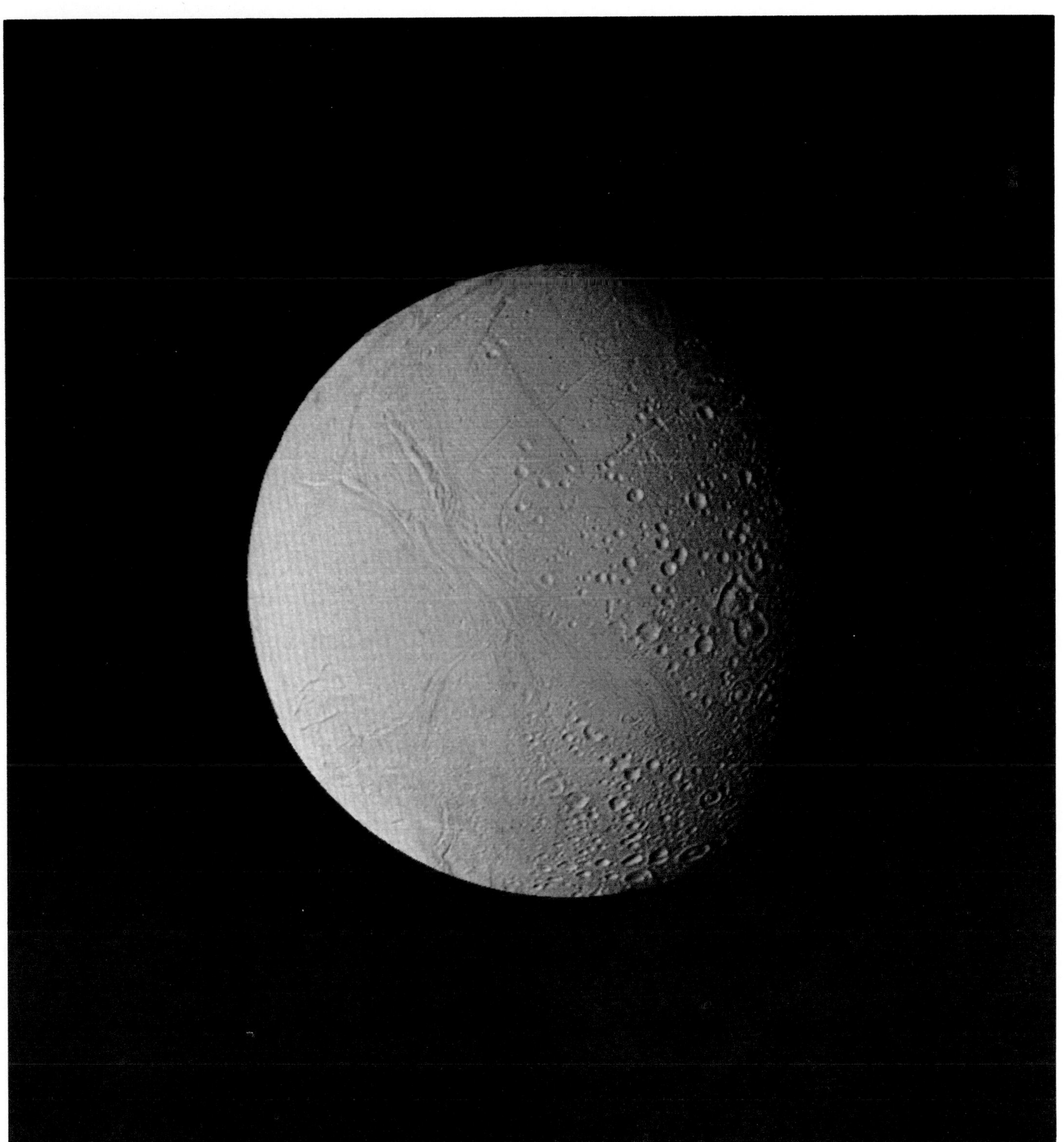

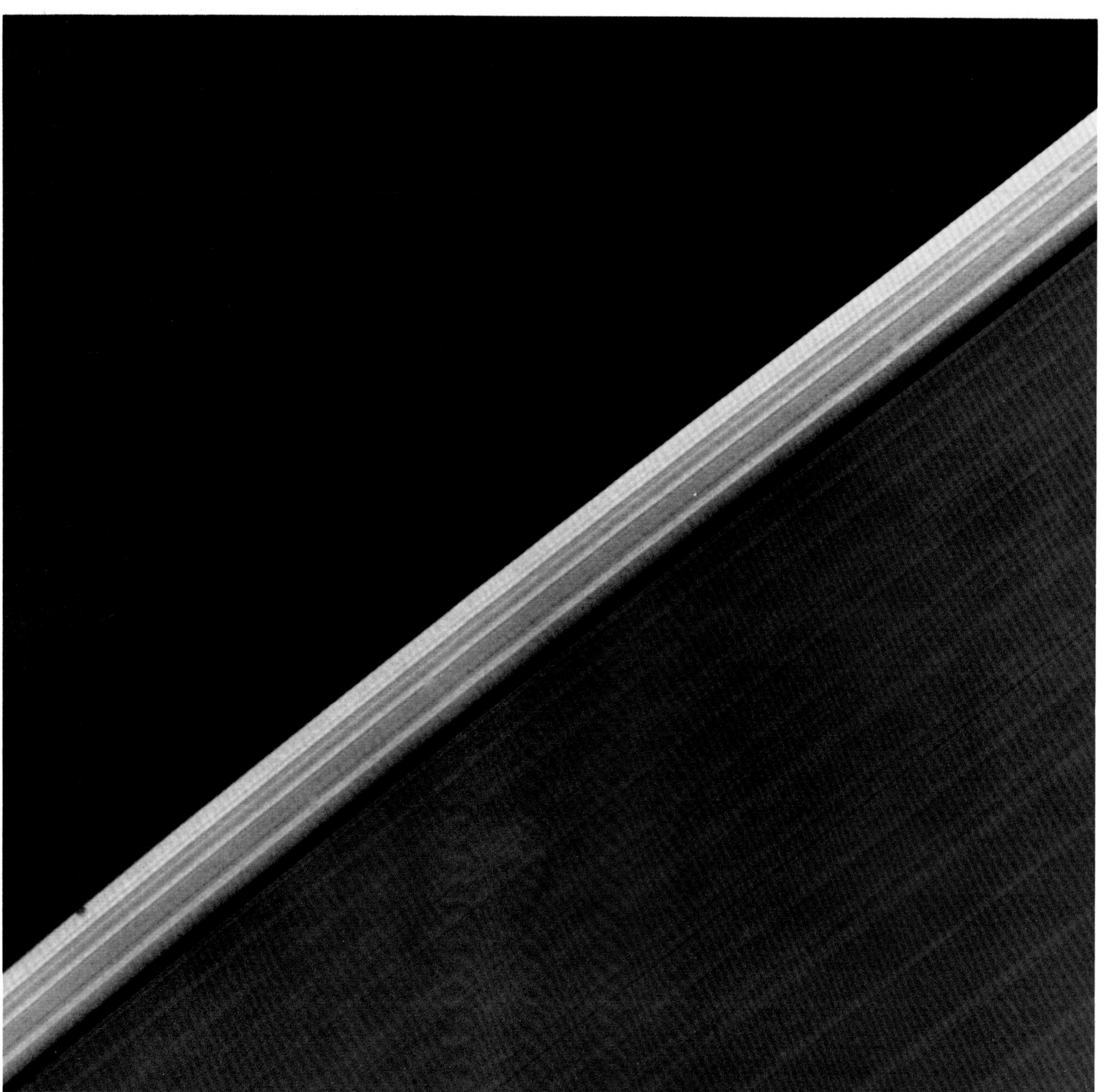

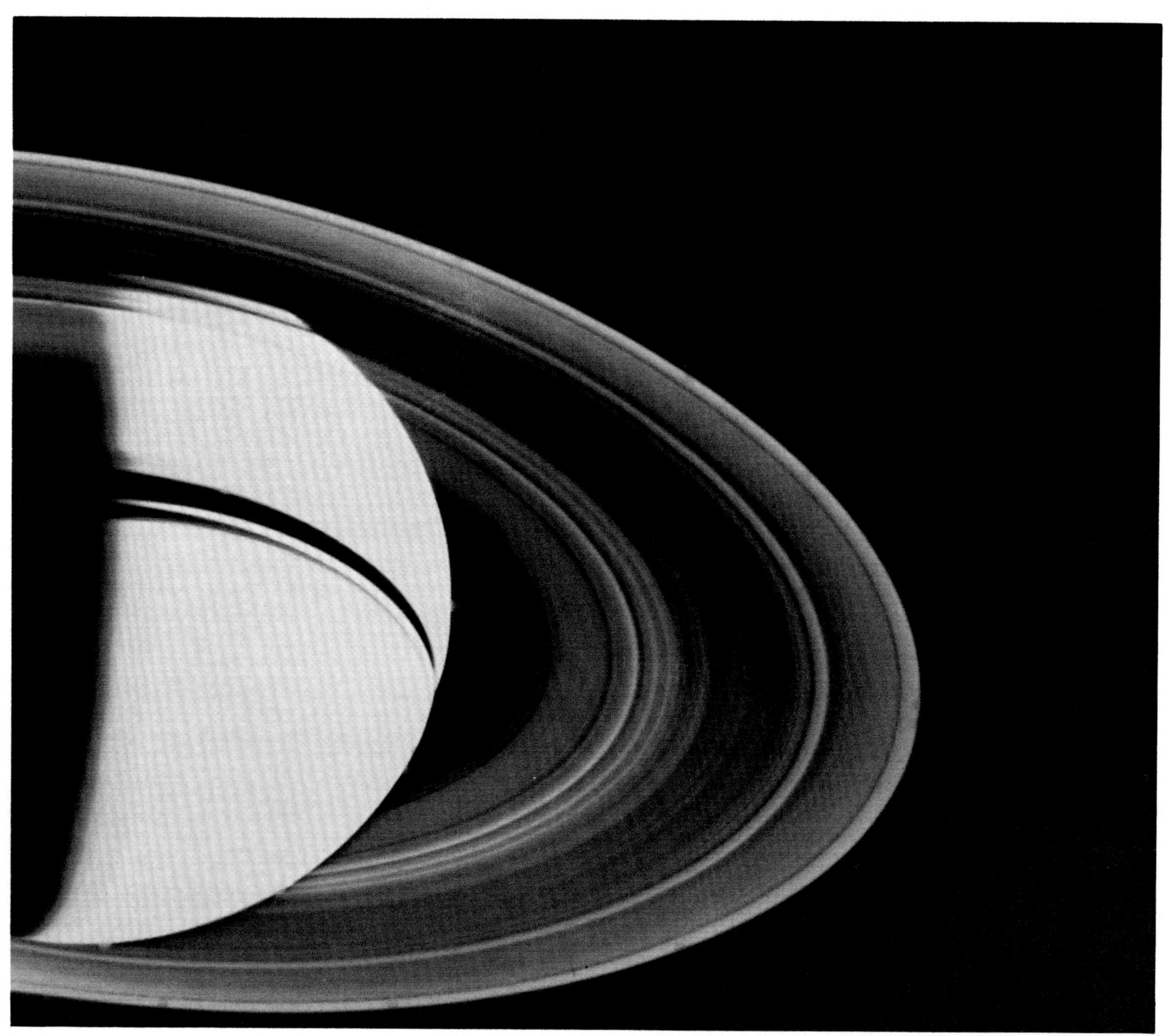

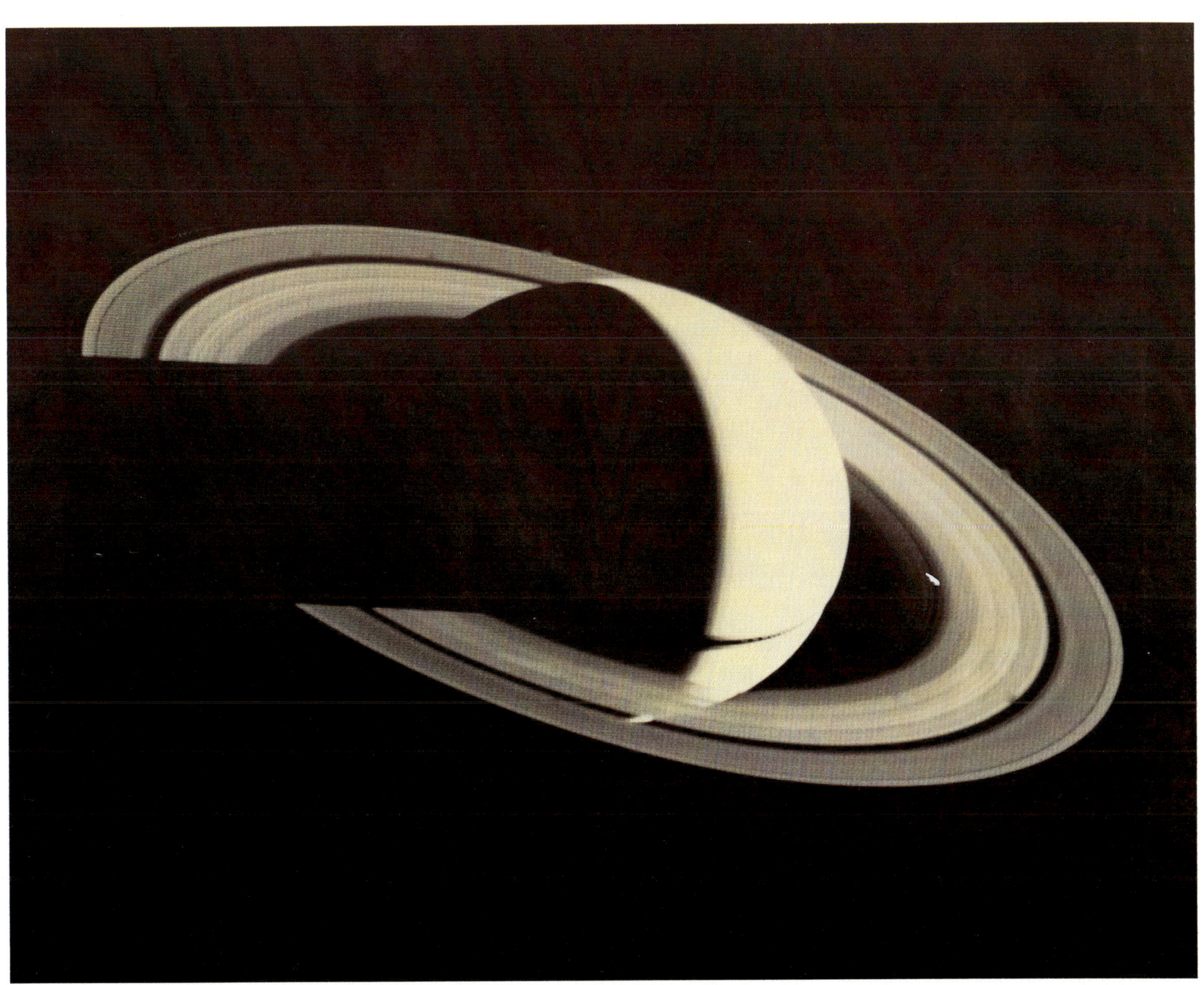

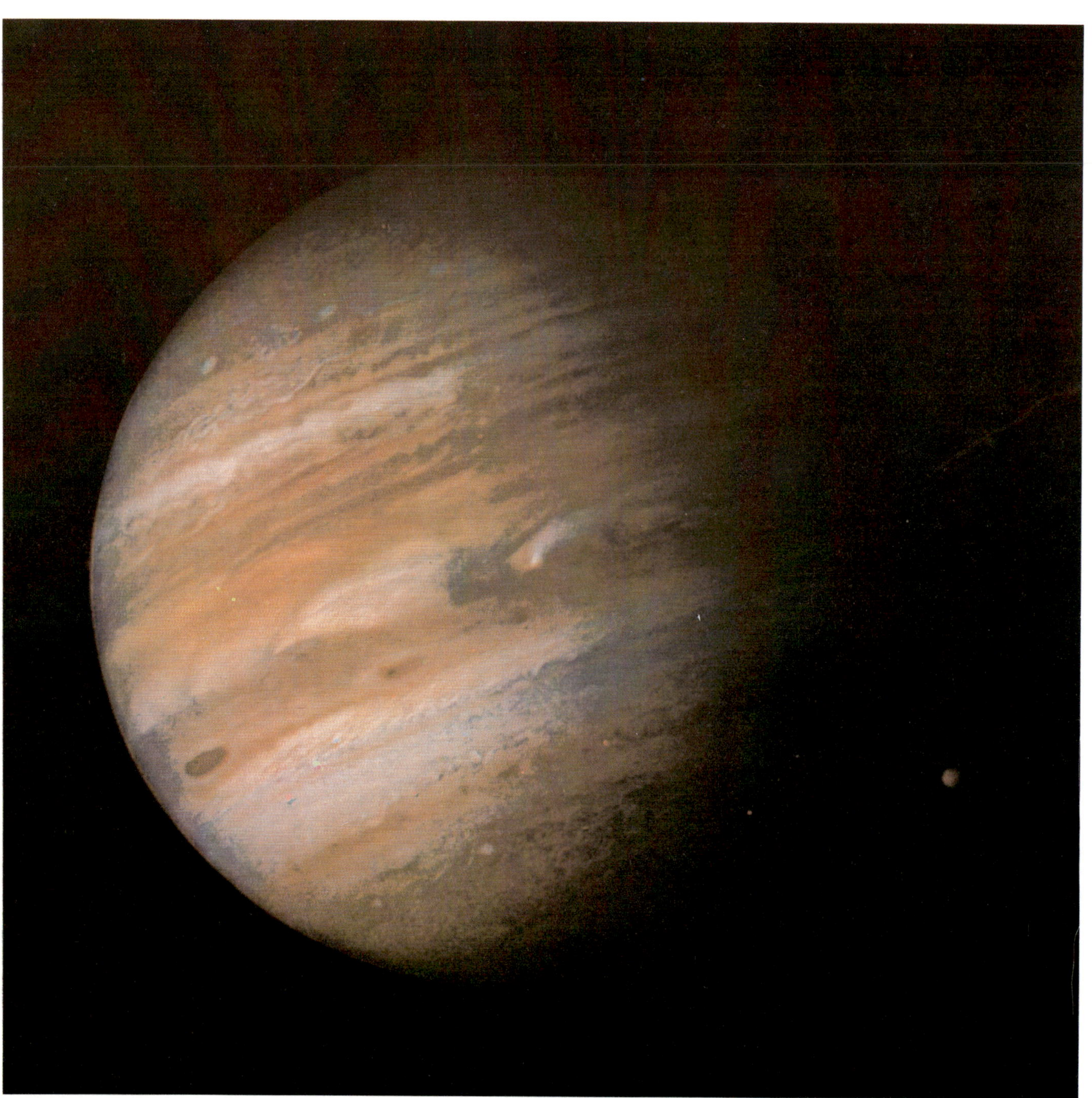

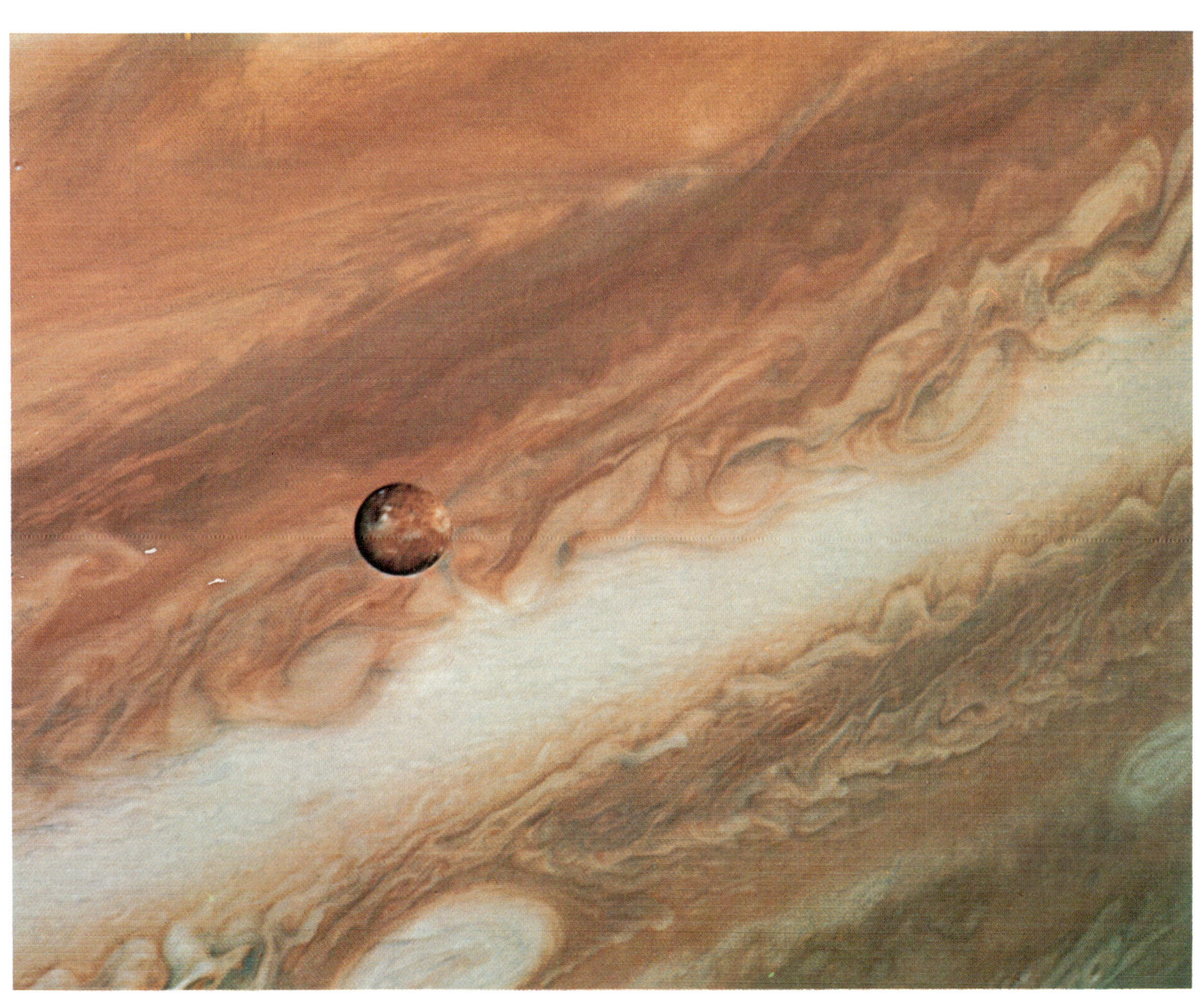

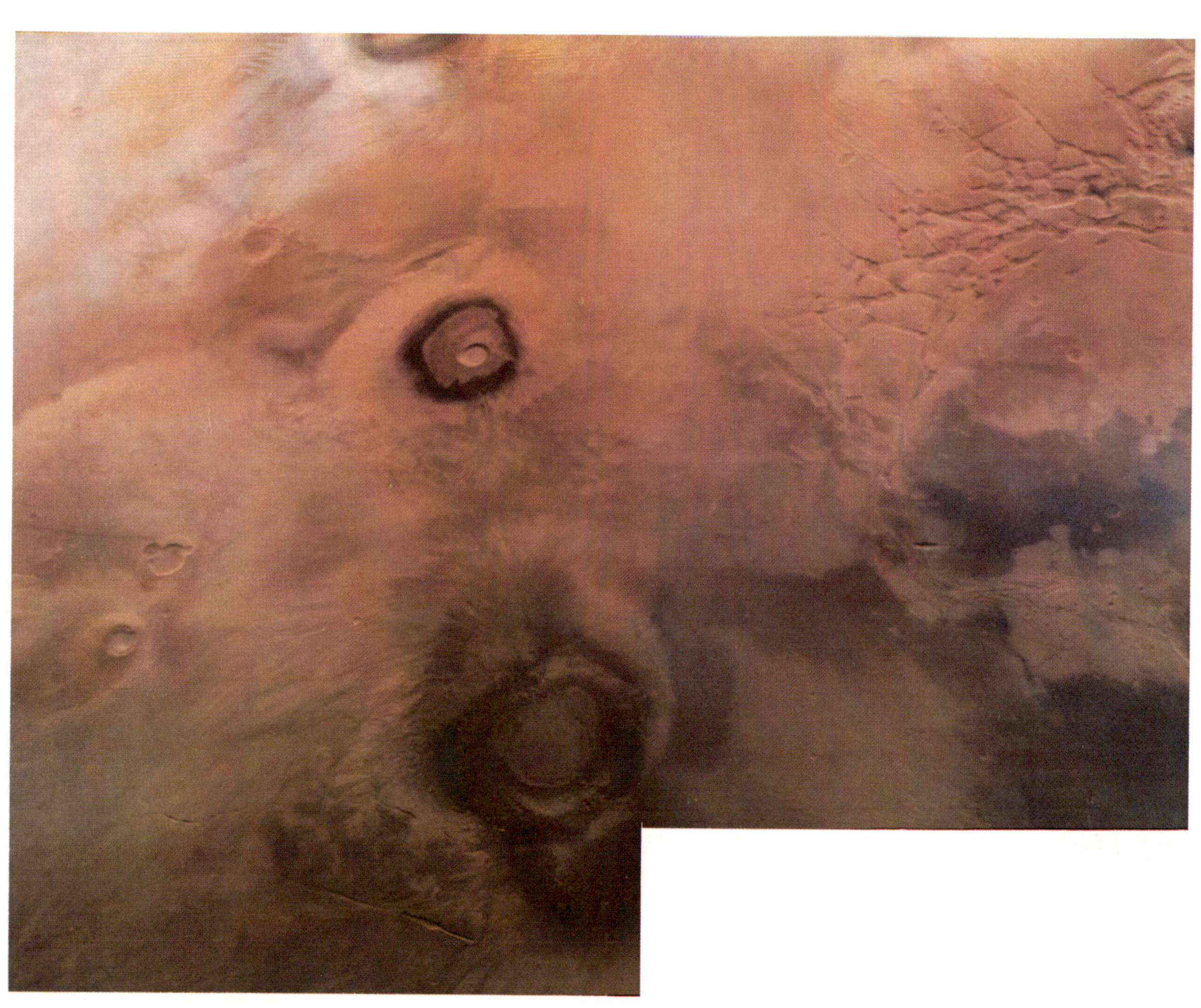

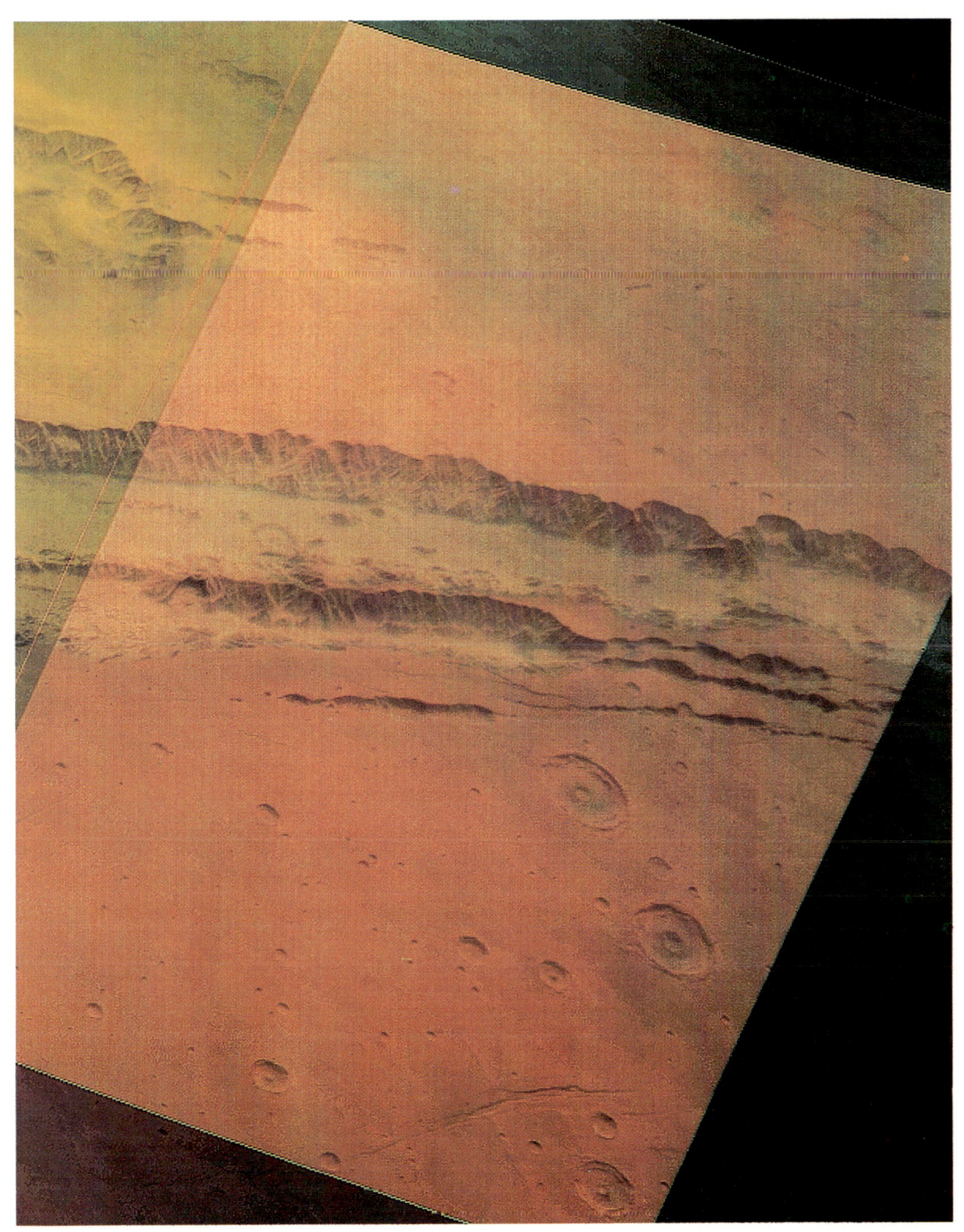

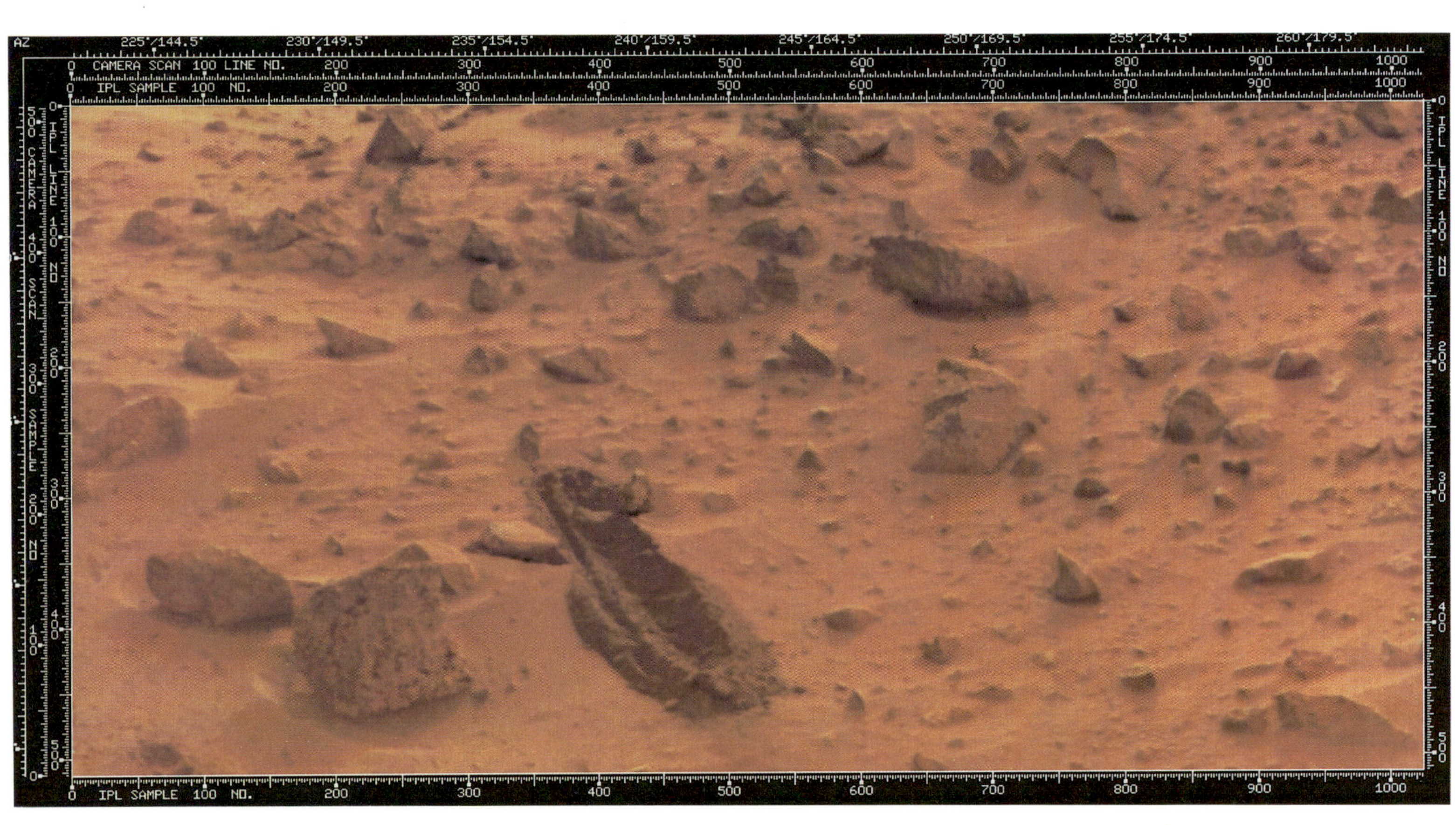
AZ
225°/144.5°
230°/149.5°
235°/154.5°
240°/159.5°
245°/164.5°
250°/169.5°
255°/174.5°
260°/179.5°
0 CAMERA SCAN 100 LINE NO. 200 300 400 500 600 700 800 900 1000
0 IPL SAMPLE 100 NO. 200 300 400 500 600 700 800 900 1000
500 CAMERA 400 SCAN 300 SAMPLE 200 NO 100 0
0 IPL LINE 100 NO 200 300 400 500
0 IPL LINE 100 NO 200 300 400 500
0 IPL SAMPLE 100 NO. 200 300 400 500 600 700 800 900 1000

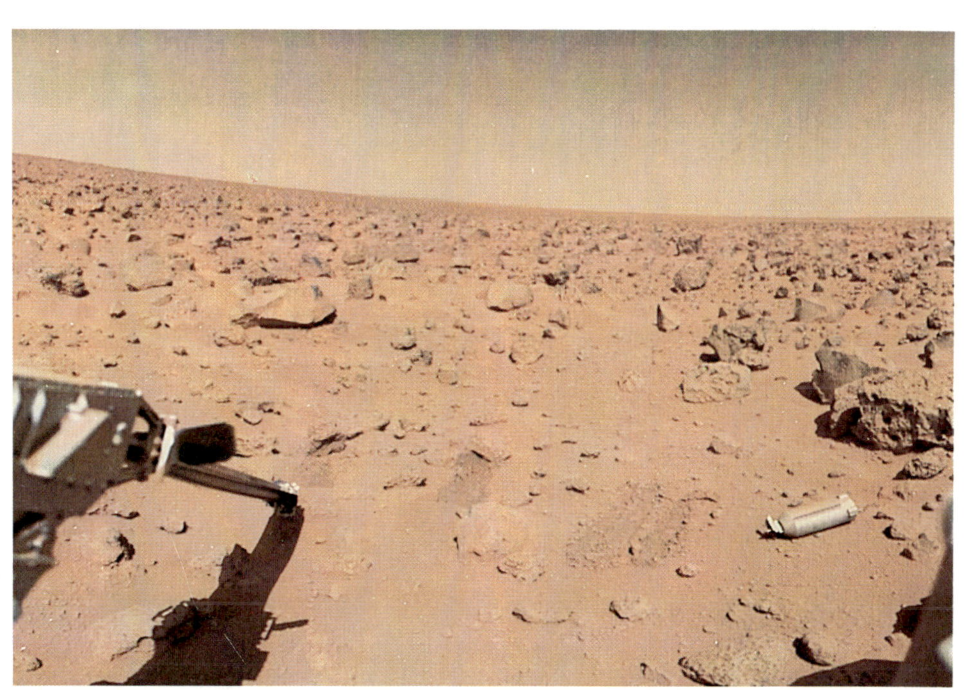

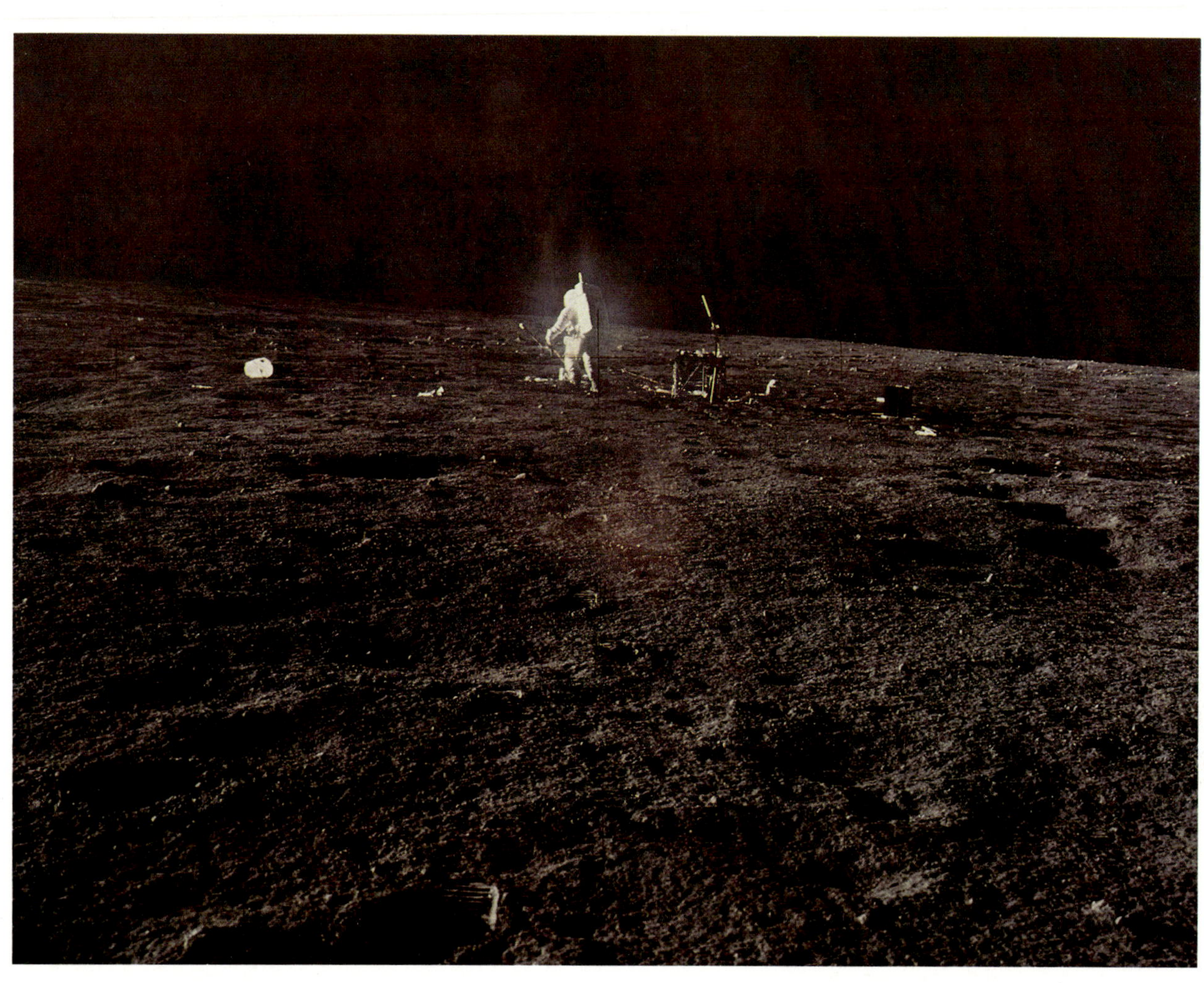

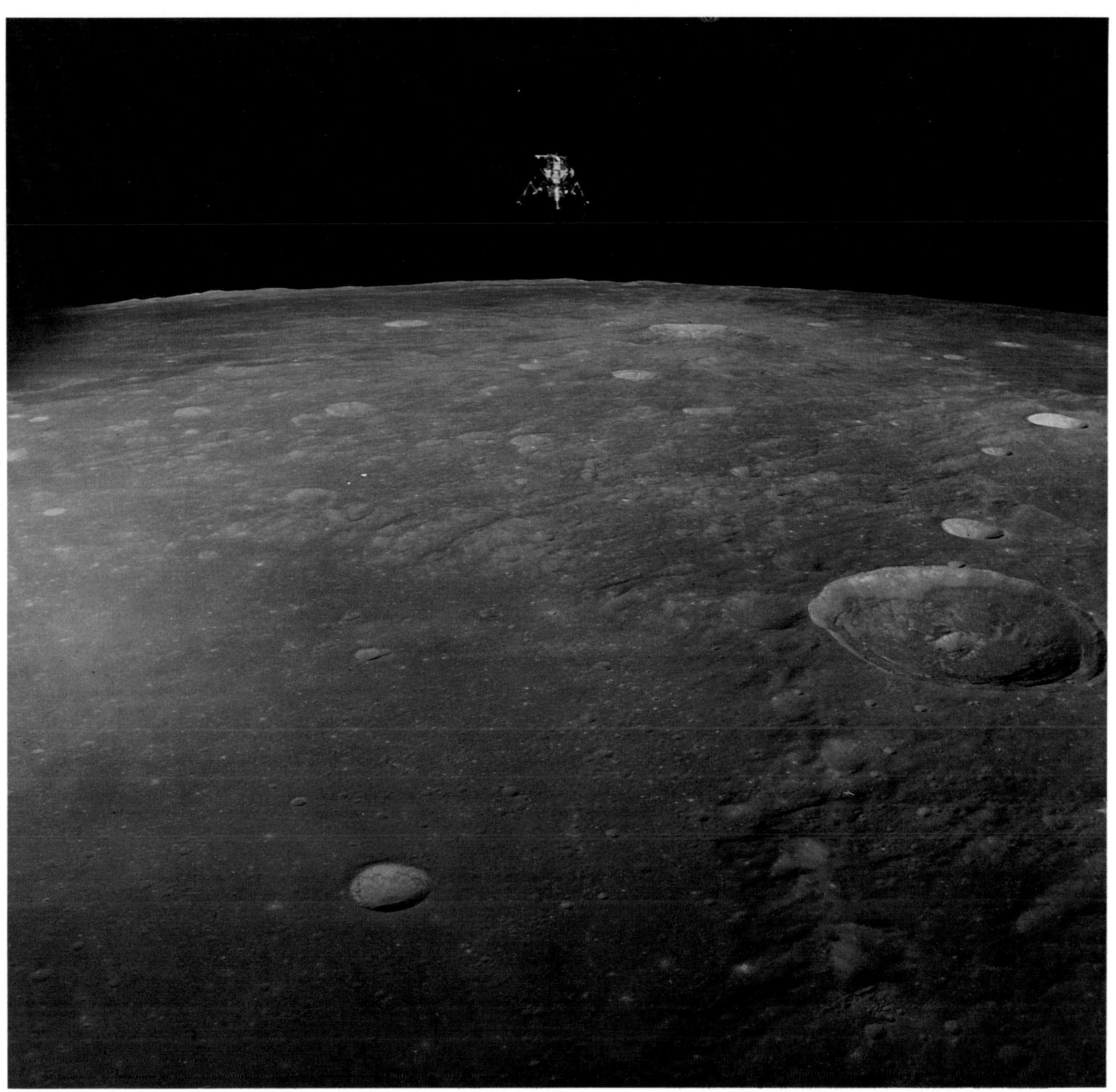

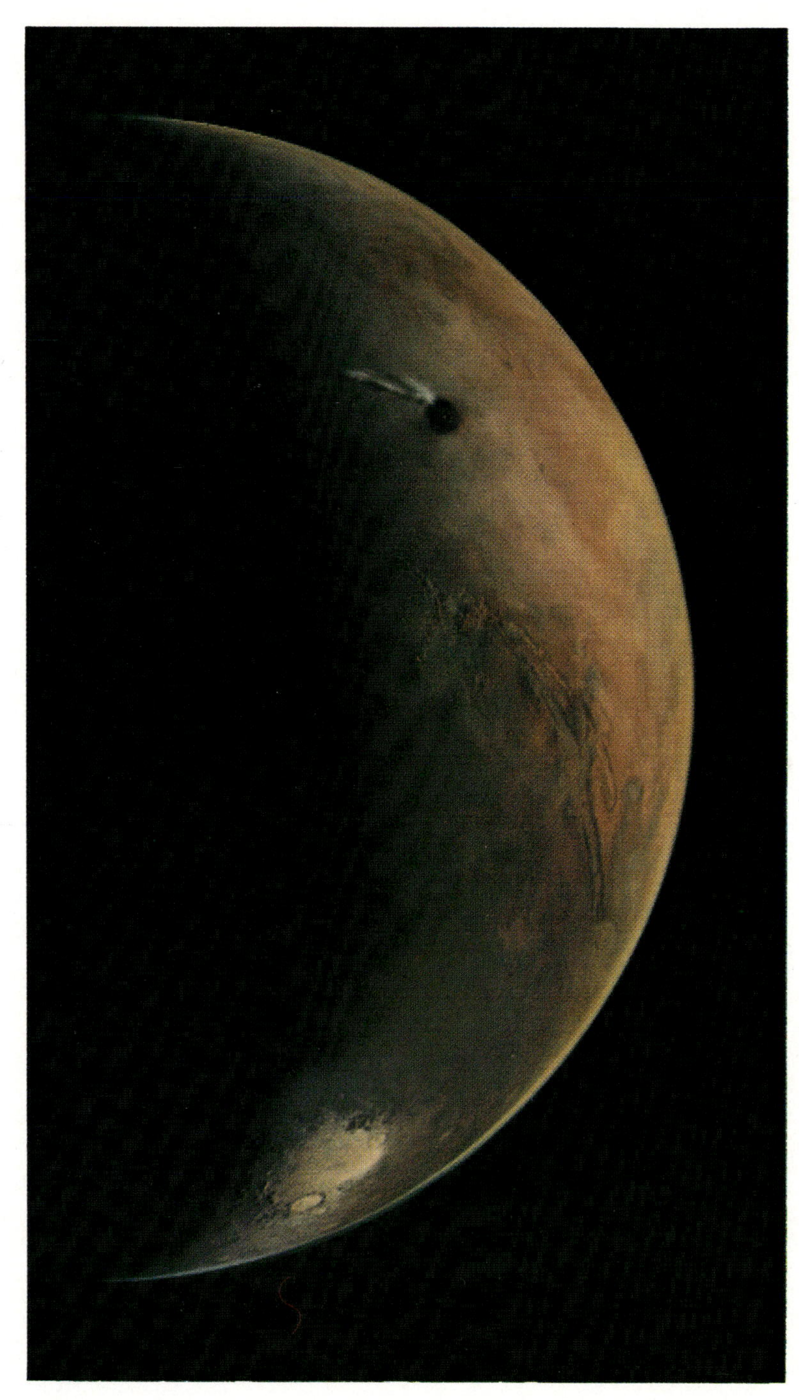

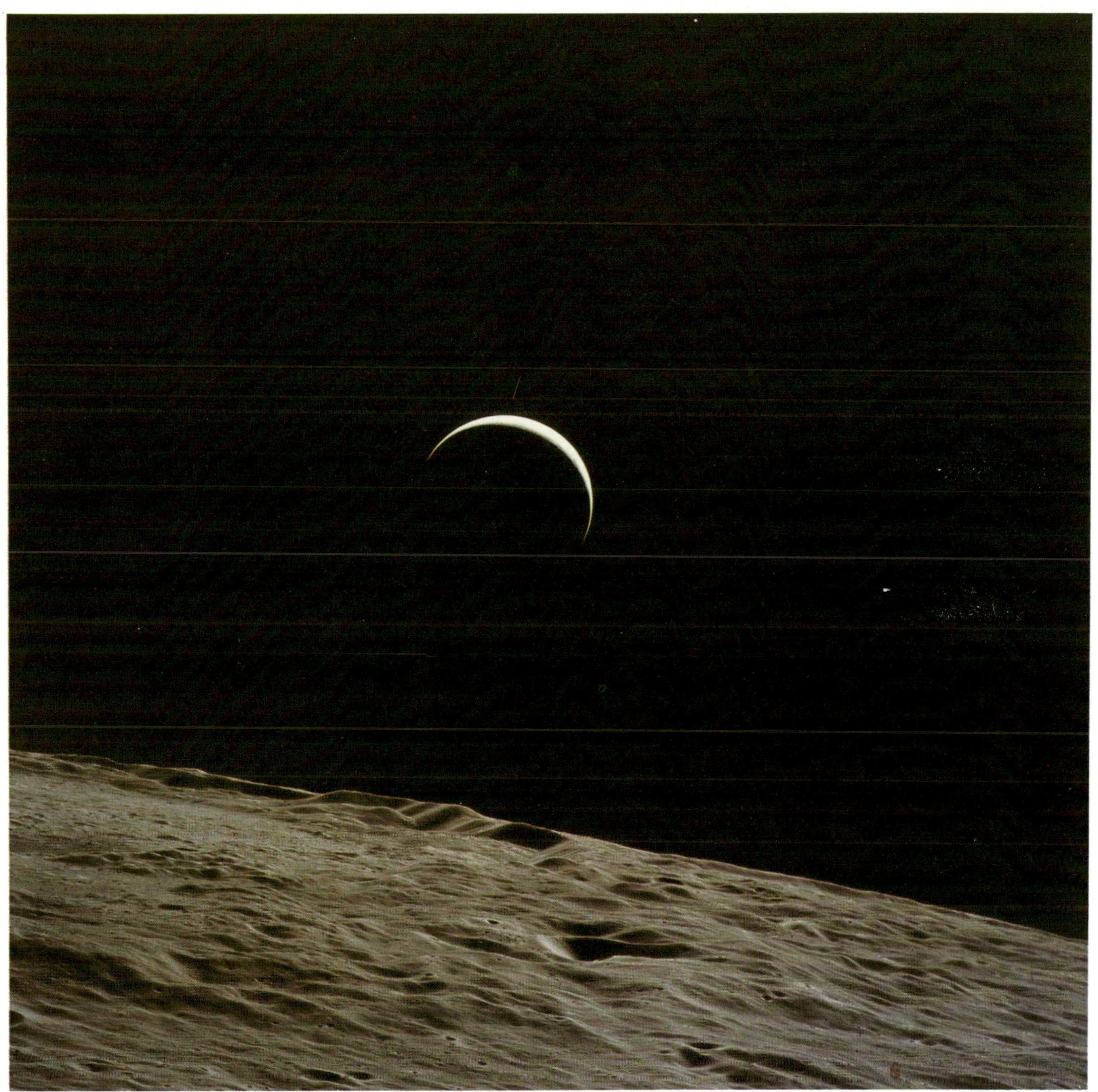

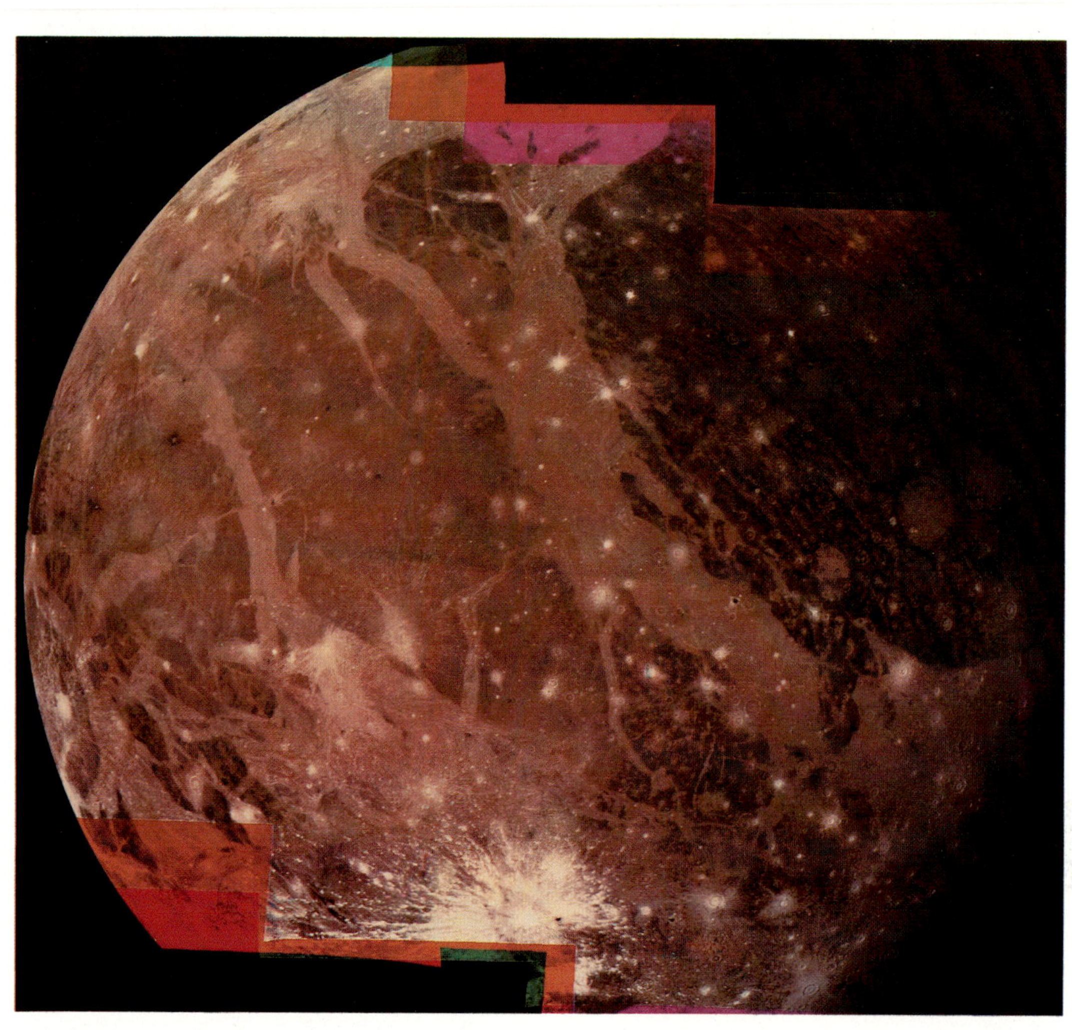

92 COMPOSITE VIEW, GANYMEDE, MOON OF JUPITER

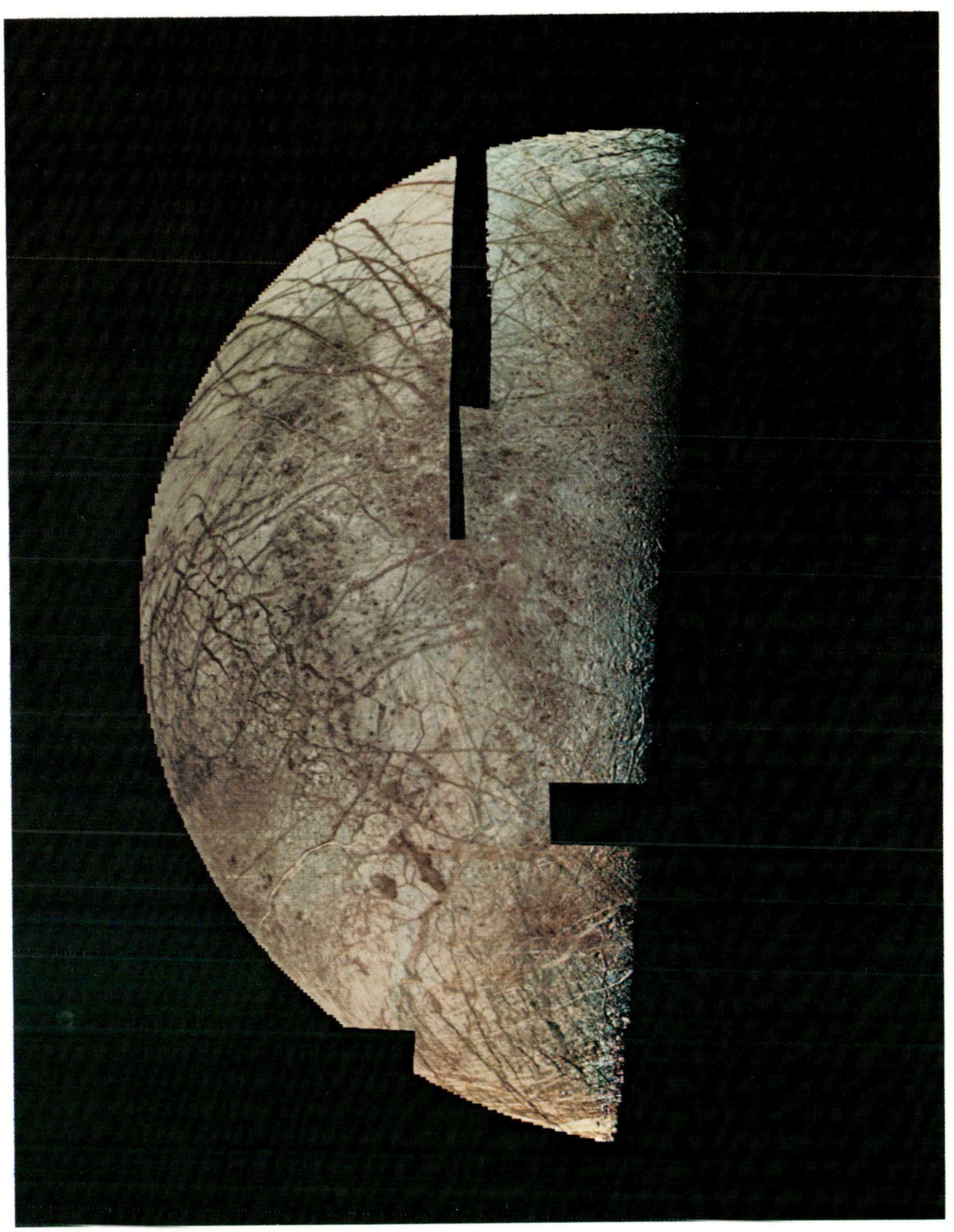

COMPOSITE VIEW, EUROPA, MOON OF JUPITER

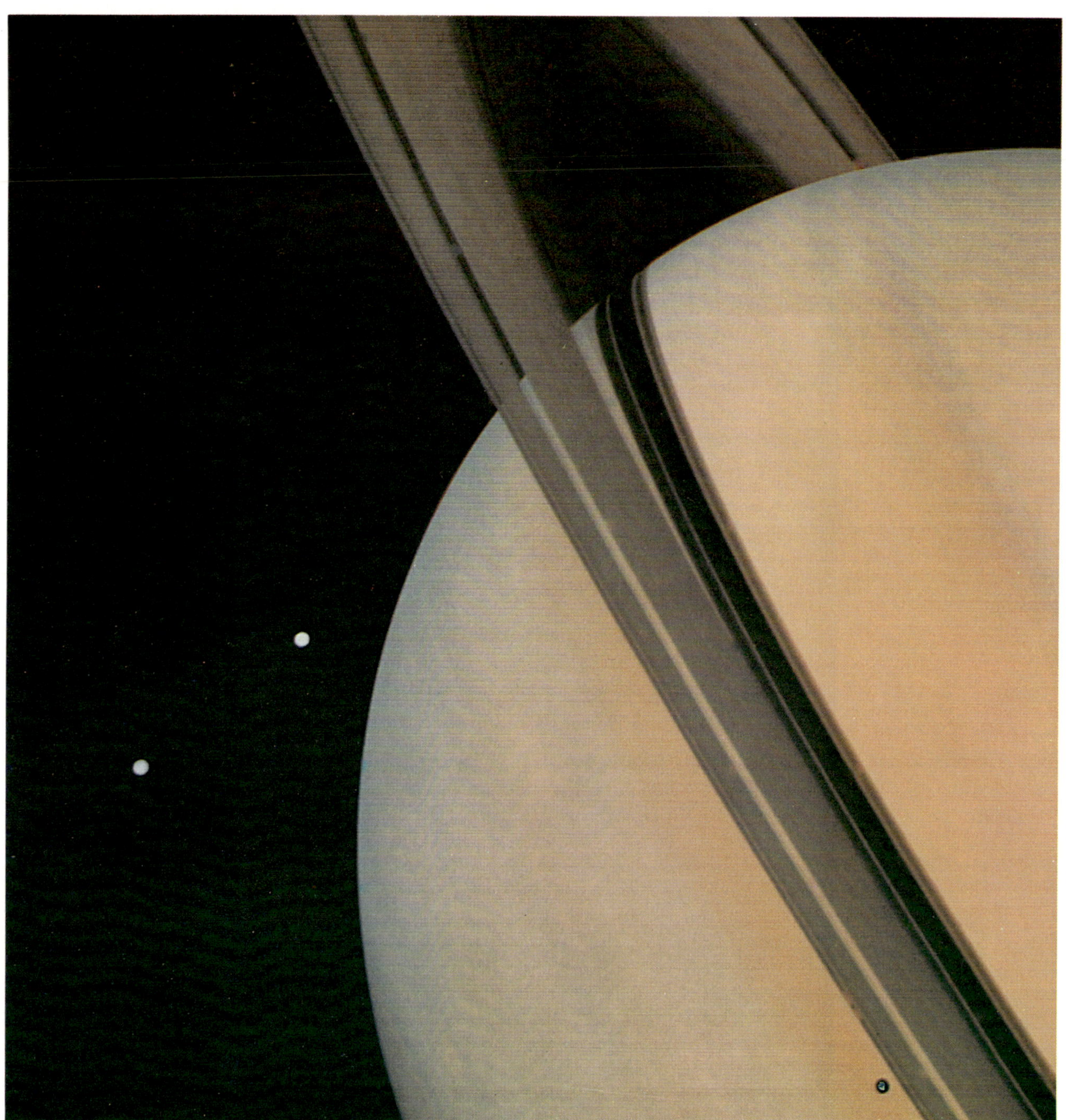

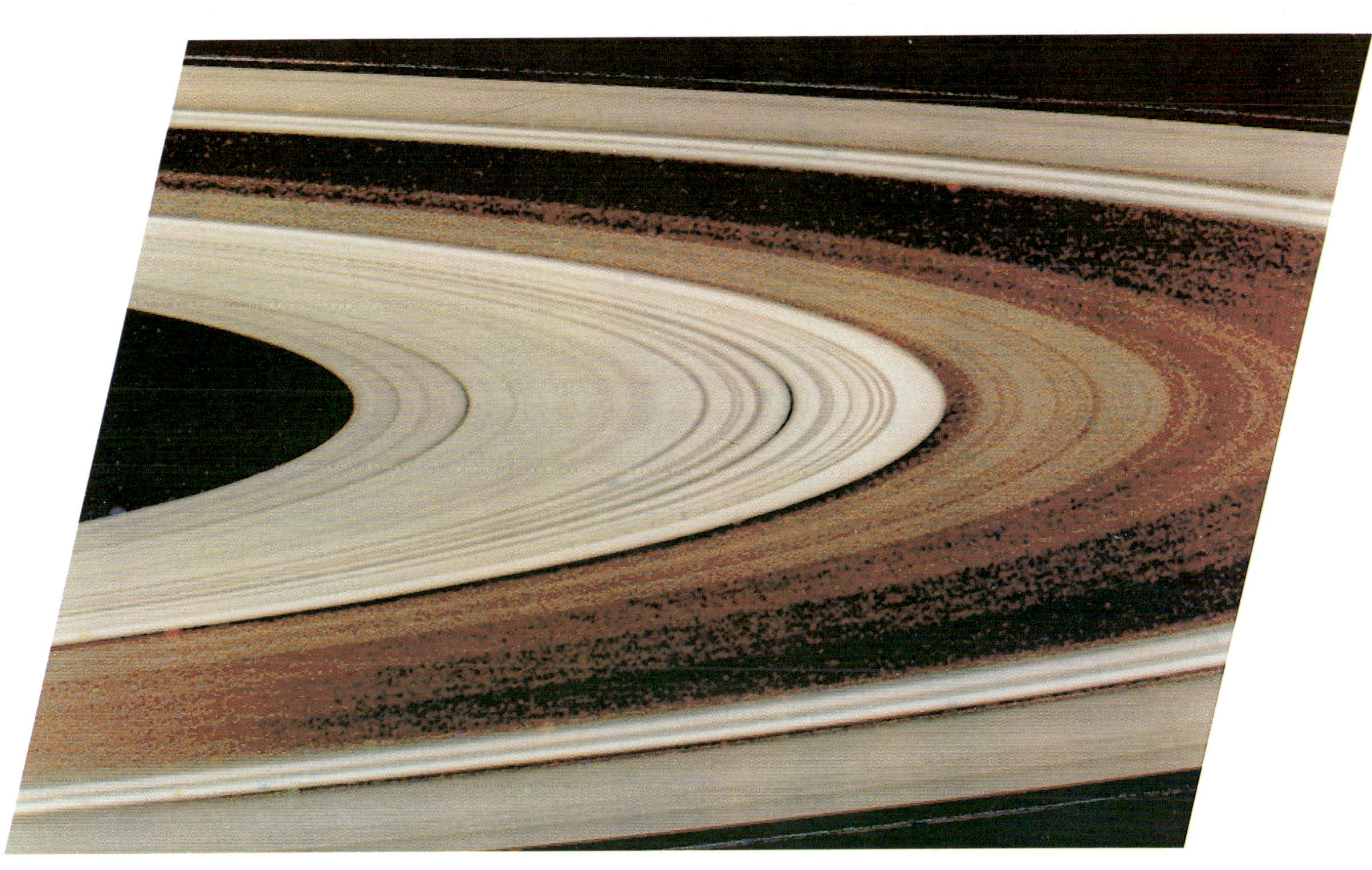

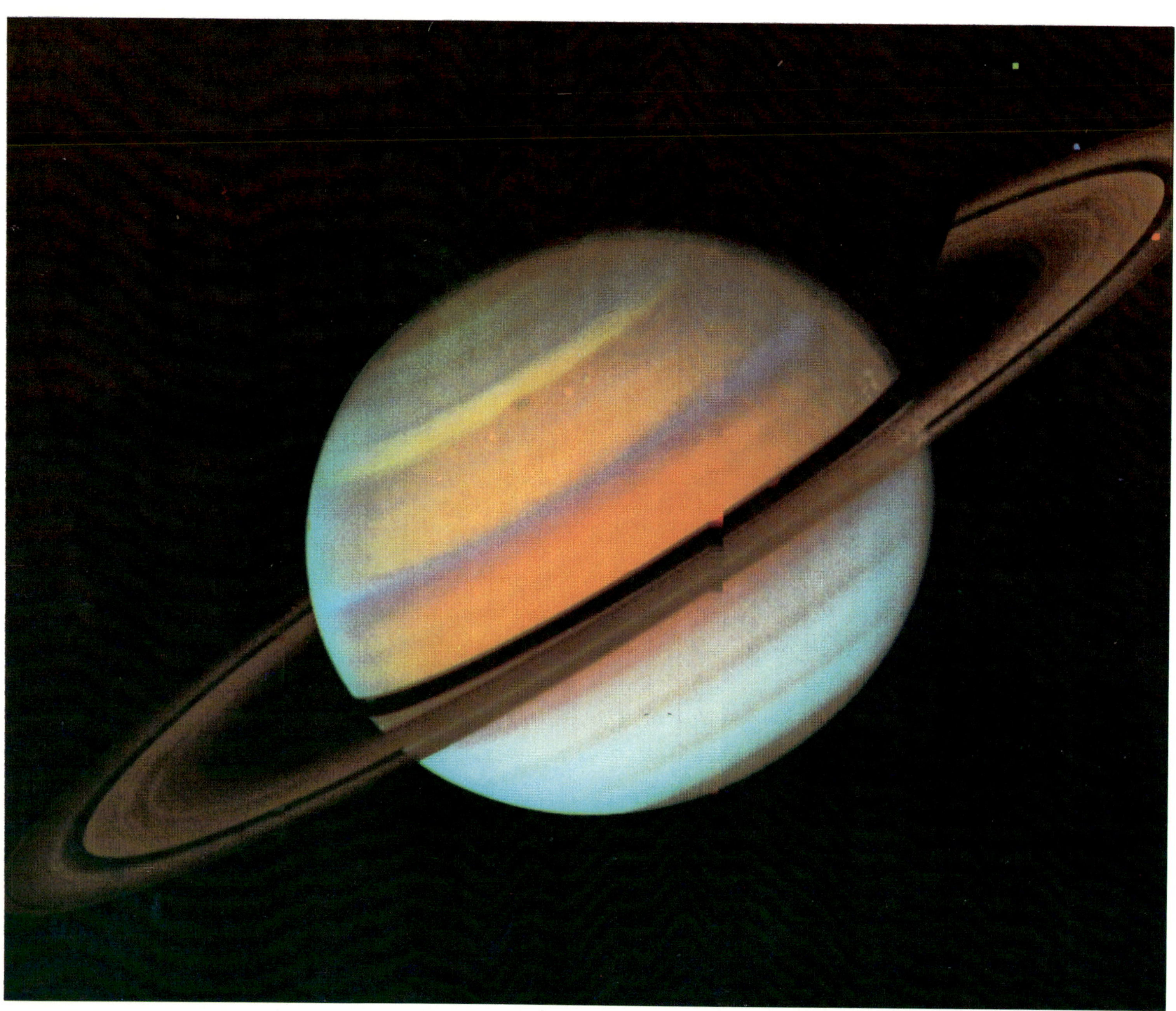

96 SATURN, BACK VIEW

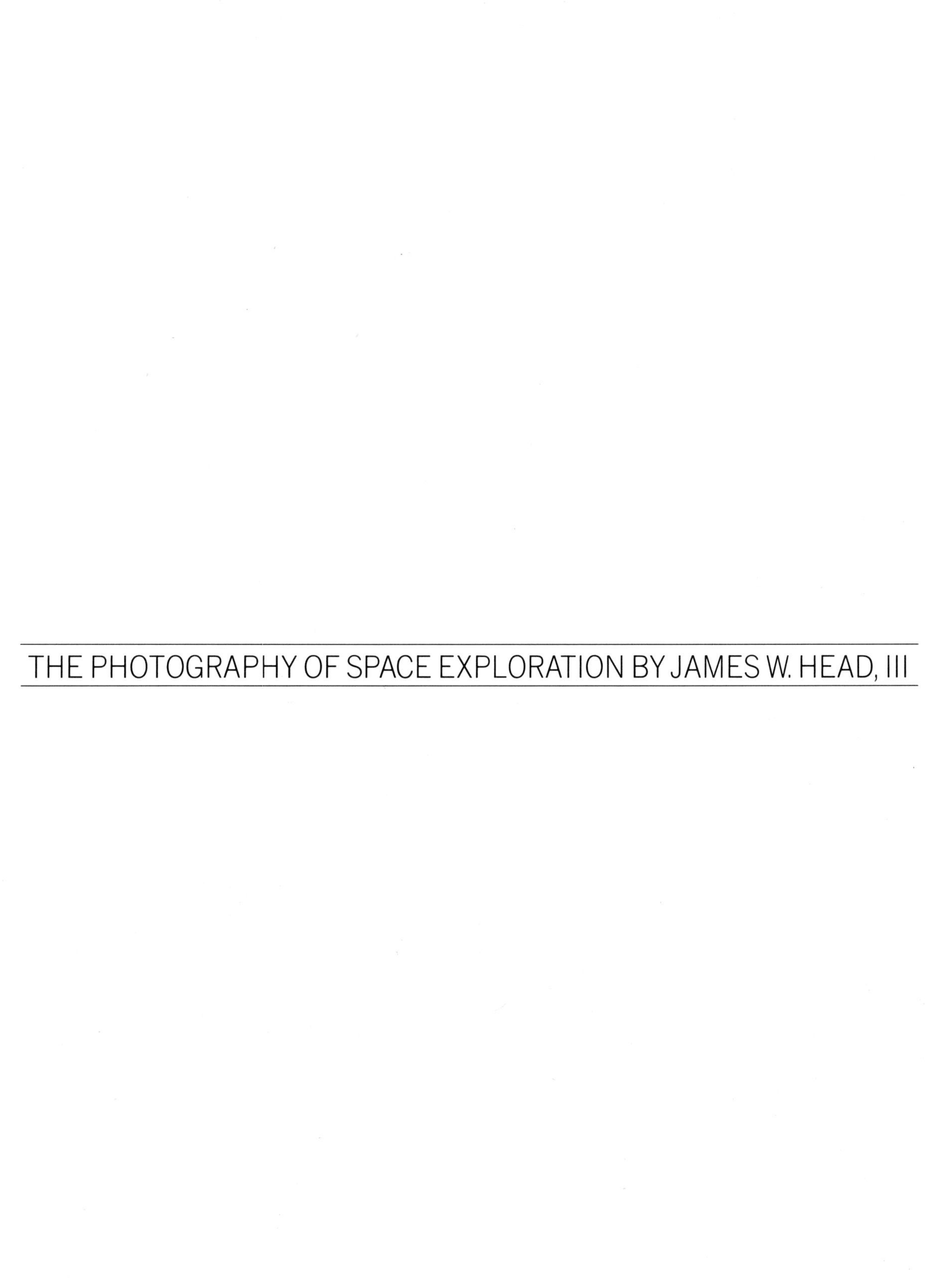

THE PHOTOGRAPHY OF SPACE EXPLORATION BY JAMES W. HEAD, III

Exploration of major physical frontiers has been done by only a few: pioneers, adventurers, sailors, mountaineers, astronauts. Early accounts of these adventures became part of the oral and written tradition. Eventually, artists, illustrators, and mapmakers accompanied many expeditions, producing a different perspective to be shared by more and more people.

The exploration of space and major technological advances have made us all explorers of the cosmos. We have witnessed the marvels of other worlds—craters on the Moon, huge canyons on Mars, active volcanoes on Io, and the enigmatic rings of Saturn. The exploration of space involves a complex set of goals and objectives: technological, scientific, engineering, and national.

In the last century, cameras have provided a way in which the visual aspects of exploration can be recorded and shared by millions; from Antarctica to the pages of periodicals in a matter of months, from Jupiter to the front page of the newspaper in a day, from Saturn to the television screen in minutes.

Thus, the role of the photographer has ranged from direct participant, as with the Apollo astronauts, to a very distant role in the case of the automated deep space probe, where a decision to obtain an image sets in motion a complex operation involving many hundreds of people so that commands can ultimately be sent millions of miles to the spacecraft. These tremendous ranges of distances and levels of involvement have provided exciting challenges to the mind and senses. Many of the things we take for granted when we photograph our surroundings on Earth, such as lighting, scale, color, perspective, and time, can be wildly different on the Moon and planets.

Sunlight, for example, varies in intensity in relation to the distance from the sun. A Voyager spacecraft, launched from Earth, looks back and obtains an image of the Earth-Moon system. As it hurtles by Jupiter and its moons, the sun's intensity has dwindled to only four percent of its value at Earth. As the same spacecraft passes Saturn, the level has decreased to one percent and the sun appears a a very tiny, very bright light in the black sky.

Atmospheric influences on lighting are very familiar to us on Earth—clouds, haze, twilight. On Mars the atmosphere is only one hundredth the density of the Earth's atmosphere at the surface. On Venus it is one hundred times more dense. Anticipating this, the Soviet spacecraft that descended to the surface of Venus carried floodlights in case the surface was too dark to obtain pictures. The Moon has no atmosphere; the lighting is harsh, the shadowing stark, but there is beauty in the unfamiliar variations. When the astronauts stood with their backs to the sun, the surface in front of them was unshadowed and appeared as a bright, washed-out spot. As they turned from side to side the shadows formed by craters, hills and mountains became more prominent and the terrain developed the character so well described by the Apollo explorers. NASA carefully chose the time of a lunar landing so that the sun was low enough in the sky to make the shadowed terrain of the landing site familiar to the astronauts piloting the spacecraft to the lunar surface. Since each earth day the astronauts remained on the moon is only one twenty-eighth of a lunar day they observed neither sunrise nor sunset from the lunar surface.

After the astronauts returned to lunar orbit, however, the situation was entirely different. The speed of the orbiting spacecraft allowed them to experience a whole range of sensations. David Scott, commander of the Apollo 15 mission, has beautifully described the sensations of a trip around the Moon. Half the Moon is saturated with bright sunlight. As the spacecraft approaches the terminator (the line separating day from night on a planet), the shadows become longer and longer and the surface detail becomes crisper and sharper—then suddenly the surface is plunged into darkness, with the only hint of the rugged landscape below being an occasional high peak sticking up and catching the final rays of sunlight—then total darkness. There is no atmosphere to diffuse the sunlight into twilight, to ease the change from day to night.

As Dave Scott's eyes became acclimated to the darkness, he began to realize that he could actually see some features on the surface. But how could this be? What was the source of light? The surface was being illuminated by earthlight—sunlight reflected off the Earth and onto the Moon. Armed with special film, the astronauts were able to obtain earthlight pictures of the surface. But soon the spacecraft passed around the Moon and out of view of either the Earth or the sun and the astronauts were plunged into total darkness. Distant stars beame the only source of light in the sky. And the Moon? No surface features could be detected—in fact, the only indication of the presence of the Moon was a black hole where there were no stars! The spacecraft was now moving toward sunrise—but there would be no pre-dawn glow—the first rays of sun shot like lightning bolts through the spacecraft windows and in a brief second night was over and day had begun again. But the show was not yet over—as the spacecraft rounded the Moon the astronauts saw a sight that stirred their most basic emotions—earthrise!

Space also brings new perspectives and states of mind to the explorer. Early explorers of the western United States saw mountains that differed in scale and sharpness from the more familiar Appalachians—and these new mountains were indeed awesome. But imagine stepping out onto a surface where landforms and scales are completely unfamiliar. Craters of all sizes and shapes cover the lunar landscape—one sees an interesting crater in the distance—but how far away is it? There are no trees, shrubs, telephone poles, or houses to provide perspective. Imagine the state of mind in which you would find yourself as you drove your moon car across this unfamiliar terrain, searching for a distant objective, with the lighting changing dramatically as you weaved in and out of craters, all the while driving as rapidly as possible to maximize the valuable time on the Moon. As you stop to explore and sample an interesting site, you wish to document the area with photographs. But experience back on Earth has shown that the bulky space suit and large helmets make conventional photographic procedures difficult. View finding, advancing film, settings, shutter activation, all appear as laborious or impossible tasks. On the Moon, your electric camera has been fitted to a bracket on your chest—you point your body, establish settings, and activate the camera with a triggered pistolgrip. And what of the well known phenomenon that all photographers have experienced upon viewing their photographs for the first time—"Well, it looked much better than this, you could see much more detail, in real life." Astronaut David Scott provided an interesting perspective on this when he described the pictures he had taken across the mile-wide lunar canyon, Hadley Rille. The pictures of the rock layers on the distant canyon wall taken with the 80 mm focal length lens fell far short of the same image in his mind. Much more comparable, he related, were those pictures he obtained using a 500 mm telephoto lens.

Many aspects of time take on new meaning in space. For the astronaut, the press of thousands of duties, goals, and objectives to be accomplished in the short period of time in space makes time for observation and reflection a luxury. Photographic images are required to document all aspects of a space mission—yet the astronauts still found time to explore and document many awe-inspiring sights. Time takes on a new dimension when the astronaut's boot forms a print in the lunar soil, disturbing material for the first time in hundreds of millions of years. Upon leaving the lunar surface the astronaut knows that these footsteps will remain undisturbed for countless thousands of years. Might these few footprints be the only surviving record of human civilization in the millenia to come?

But the Moon is nearby. What of time in deeper space? The short delay of radio communication in near-Earth space stretches into minutes. The radio-signal command to take a picture travels for 80 minutes before reaching the Voyager spacecraft at Saturn. When the Viking lander touched down on the surface of Mars in 1976, it had been previously instructed to immediately take a picture of the surface and transmit it back to Earth. Imagine the tension as we sat before the TV screens waiting 18 minutes for this picture to travel from Mars—almost paralyzed with the knowledge that the landing, be it a destructive crash or a safe touchdown, was a fait accompli.

Space exploration also changes our earthbound perspective about color. Our atmosphere causes the Earth's sky to appear blue. The lunar sky, with no atmosphere, is the color of deep space, black. But what of Mars? How do we interpret colors using camera systems far less sophisticated than the human eye? The Viking landers carried color charts on the side of the spacecraft so that the cameras could photograph them and make comparisons to colors on the surface and in the sky. The martian sky appears pinkish due to the suspended particles of red dust in the tenuous atmosphere.

The vast range of distance, temperature, light, and atmospheric effects encountered in space require a tremendous diversity of techniques to record exploration. For example, the astronauts returned the film they exposed on the Moon to the Earth for processing. Most spacecraft, however, do not return to Earth and sophisticated techniques are required to return the images. The Lunar Orbiter spacecraft developed its film on board the spacecraft, electronically scanned the developed image, and faithfully transmitted the image (including the occasional bimat bubbles) back to Earth, where it was reconstructed and printed. The Mariner spacecraft looked at the planets with a television camera. The images were converted to digital form and sent back to Earth as a stream of numbers. For the Mariner 9 images of Mars, each picture contained 700 lines, each line contained 832 picture elements (nicknamed pixels), and for each pixel 512 levels of brightness could be measured by nine-bit digitization of the signal returning to Earth. Each picture we hold in our hands consists of over five million bits of information.

Conventional photography records the scene observed only in visible light. How then can we expect to see the surface of a cloud-shrouded planet such as Venus? Technological advances in the last few decades have enabled us to obtain images at a variety of wavelengths both longer and shorter than those observed by the eye. For example, imaging systems designed to operate at radar wavelengths have been used to penetrate Venus' thick cloud cover and take pictures of the surface. This procedure is interestingly analogous to studio lighting in that the "light" source (the radar transmitter) can be oriented in relation to the subject to be "photographed." Images of planetary surfaces at these and other wavelengths allow us to see with different sets of eyes, and let us appreciate how other life forms might perceive and explore their environment.

Exploration and discovery are fundamental aspects of history and human existence. Indeed, the major milestones of history can be viewed as a series of events in the exploration of the mind and environment. Despite the human propensity for inertia, it seems that change is truly the essence of life. This need for change seems to be a major motivator for exploration and discovery.

The last two decades of space exploration and discovery have challenged us and changed our perspective on ourselves and our place in the solar system. It has forced us to redefine our environment and, a little bit at a time, to modify the framework in which we view everything in our daily lives. The magnificent images of space, more than everything else, have made us all explorers of the cosmos and ourselves.

JAMES HEAD IS PROFESSOR OF PLANETARY GEOLOGY AT BROWN UNIVERSITY AND HAS BEEN DEEPLY INVOLVED IN THE NASA PROGRAMS TO EXPLORE THE MOON AND MARS. HE IS PRESENTLY HELPING TO PLAN FOR THE NEXT GENERATION OF SPACECRAFT TO FLY TO JUPITER.